Arab/American

Arab/American

Landscape, Culture, and Cuisine in Two Great Deserts

GARY PAUL NABHAN

The University of Arizona Press   Tucson

The University of Arizona Press
© 2008 Gary Paul Nabhan
All rights reserved

Library of Congress Cataloging-in-Publication Data appear on the
last printed page of this book.

Manufactured in Canada on acid-free, archival-quality paper
containing 100% postconsumer waste and processed chlorine free.
13 12 11 10 09 08   6 5 4 3 2 1

Are There Arabs Amongst Us?
A Legend from the Chihuahuan Desert

One hot summer day nearly a century ago, a number of Mexican men assembled outside a little cantina in a desert pueblo not far south of the U.S. border. Just as soon as the bartender opened the door, they went in and ordered drinks to quench their thirst. After all of them had downed the first round, they looked around to see if anyone new to the scene was there. They noticed one stranger in their midst. Although he had on much the same dress as they did, he didn't exactly look like he was one of their kind.

"Who might you be?" they asked. "You don't look Mexican. . . . In fact, you look a little like pictures we've seen of Arabs!"

"No, I'm just a Mexican, a Mexican citizen, in fact," the man said and went on drinking, his hat pulled low over his eyes.

They paid him little more mind until one of their gang offered a toast. "¡Viva Villa! May he become our next president!"

All the men raised their drinks and shouted "¡Ojalá!" except for the stranger, who shouted, "¡Insha'alla!"

The men turned and looked at him again. "You're no Mexican!" they yelled, confronting him. "You're an Arab masquerading as a Mexican!"

"That's not true," the stranger retorted. "And just to prove to you that I'm a Mexican, I'll sing you my favorite corrido ballad from my very first days helping you fight for the revolution: *Pancho Villa got ready to ride, mounting his camel's dark hide. . . .*"

—Translated from a story recounted by Trinidad Chavez Rodriguez of
   Yoquivo, Chihuahua, April 2007

Contents

Photographs by Gary Paul Nabhan follow page 54

Acknowledgments

During the writing of this book, I have been a guest in the kitchens, terraced gardens, date plantations, and libraries of many more people than I can possibly name here. They have offered me far more than a cup of Arabic coffee with cardamom or a glass of mint tea. I remain grateful for their stories, ideas, commentaries, and goodwill. I thank especially my cousins in Kfar Zabad and Zahle, Lebanon, including Shibley Nabhan and his family, Victor Nabhan and his family, Najim Nabhan and his family, and Dalia Al Jawhary. In Beirut, Kamal Mouzawak, Rami Zurayk, and John Waterbury graciously hosted me. In Muscat, Oman, I was made welcome by the fine scientist Dr. Sulaiman Al-Khanjari, Ali Masoud Al-Subhi, and their friends at Sultan Qaboos University. In Siwa, Egypt, the goodwill of Mahdi el-Hewety, Fathi Malim, Ahmed Jerry Hammam, and Omar Ahmed Ali were essential to my work. In Jerusalem, I was blessed by the inspiration, hospitality, and food provided by Kevork Alemian and Moshe Basson, two of the leaders of Chefs for Peace.

My traveling companions for these journeys have been many, and their insights greatly shaped these stories. My wife, Laurie; our children, Laura Rose and Jeremy; and my brothers, Douglas and Norman, were great comrades on the road in Lebanon, Egypt, and Oman. David Cavagnaro and Father Dave Denny accompanied me on separate trips to Egypt. Many folks—including Candelaria Orosco, Ofelia Zepeda, Fillman Bell, Lorraine Eiler, Wendy Hodgson, Caroline Wilson, Peggy Olwell, Jim Hills, Amadeo Rea, Bill Broyles, Susan Zwinger, Larry Stevens, Humberto Suzan, Tom Sheridan, and Paul Mirocha—have shared the trail with me in the Sonoran and Chihuahuan deserts. My daughter, Laura, was my guide to the Lebanese families and restaurants of Merida and the Yucatán Peninsula. Her godmother, the late Laura Kerman, introduced me to the legacy of Robert Forbes, and her own legacy has left a lasting imprint on me as well.

I have been fortunate to get to know as friends some of the great scholars whose interests bridge the gulf between Arabian and American *deserta*. I have been both inspired and informed by Naomi Shihab Nye, Greg Orfalea, Habeeb Salloum, Estevan Arellano, Rick Bayless, Kamal Mouzawak, Tony Burgess, Bill Dunmire, and Michael Bonine.

Agnese Haury has offered me insights and guidance from her own experiences in North Africa and the Near East, more than for any other project she has sponsored for me. I am honored by her enthusiasm and financial support for these efforts. Sara Jane Freymann, my literary agent, and Christine Szuter, director of the University of Arizona Press and longtime friend, did much to give this project its finesse. Patti Hartmann has been a fine editor and enthusiast. Joe Wilder, director of the Southwest Center, has also encouraged me to bridge Southwest studies with Near Eastern studies. Joe is among the several journal and magazine editors who helped these essays along when they were in their early stages. Others include Stephen Corey, Jennifer Sahn, Emerson Blake, David Seidman, Jack Shoemaker, Dick Doughty, Bruce Dingas, Bill Broyles, Richard Felger, Alison Deming, Lauret Savoy, Liza Gizzi, and Daniel Moerman. My hope is that their publications—*Georgia Review, Journal of the Southwest, Audubon, Orion, Economic Botany,* and *Saudi Aramco World*—endure for another thousand years. Jeannette Sherman, Heather Farley, and Judy Buzard patiently assisted with the horrendous logistical issues of travels in Arabian deserta.

This book is dedicated to the three folks who have shared many conversations with Laurie and me about these topics over the years: Agnese Haury, my mentor; Douglas Nabhan, my brother and fellow Arabian bibliophile; and Laura Rose Reichhardt, my daughter. And in re-reading these pages, I remember my Nabhan elders who returned to the earth during the writing of these stories: George Nabhan, Violet Hallen, Mabel Schott, Mary Wilds, and Linda Piet.

Arab/American

Introduction

What Flows Between Dry Worlds

I HAVE LIVED half my life in an American desert where I often hear echoes of messages and images emanating from halfway around the world. Those echoes come from the Arabian *deserta*: Lebanon, Syria, Jordan, Palestine, Egypt, Oman, Saudi Arabia, and Yemen. These places have been home to my Banu Nabhani ancestors and kin for millennia— places that have shaped them, as they in turn have shaped me.

Not too long ago I belatedly came to understand how many images, landscape terms, foods, crop plants, weeds, livestock breeds, and cultural traditions from the Arabian deserts have shaped lives besides my own in American deserta. Over the past decade, I have spent an increasing amount of time in what my grandfather simply called "the Old Country." While doing so, I have come to fathom my own home in an arid landscape in ways I could not have previously imagined.

After several decades of working as a desert ecologist and agricultural scientist in the deserts of the U.S. Southwest and northwestern Mexico, I was blessed with the opportunity to travel, lecture, and undertake field studies in Egypt, Oman, Palestine, Israel, Lebanon, Syria, and the United Arab Emirates. Having developed over many years an ear for the folk terms and tales rooted in arid landscapes, I listened for such elements as I traveled among Berber, Bedouin, Jewish, Armenian, and sedentary Arab tribesmen through their own homelands. As I steeped myself in these desert brews, a complex set of fragrances and flavors began to arise and were eventually imbued in the stories and commentaries given here.

It has perhaps been the oddest of times to embrace Arabian deserta as part of my heritage. The nation-state of which I have been a citizen all my life has of late been in *wars of mutual misunderstanding* with many Arab-speaking peoples. For me, it does not matter who initiated these wars or who has suffered the most from them; to achieve peace, mutual respect, and collaboration we must reach some common understandings.

At the same time, natural-resource managers in the U.S. Southwest have been in a struggle with the very desert in which they live, showing more interest in the oil or water below it than in the land itself. I have ached with grief over these misunderstandings, these wars, these struggles. And I have spent many sleepless nights wondering what one poor soul might do to heal the wounds that have ruptured among the two cultures of which I feel a part.

Because my habitual means of expression are more literary than political, I have been prompted to seek out stories that link together these two seemingly different cultures and places, rather than to dwell on those stories that may further divide them. I am inherently fascinated by bonds, not sutures. In being so inclined, I may risk slighting the gravity of the current divisions between religions, governments, economic structures, and social lifestyles, but I am willing to take that risk. I do not intend to ignore the pain and suffering that any single person, family, or community has shouldered during this era of war and violation. Nevertheless, I have tried to imagine a world in which *convivencia* (living together with others), consilience, tolerance, and peace are possible. I sense that I will fail to imagine such a world if I spend all my time drawing an artificial line in the hot desert sands. And so I have sought stories that might remind both you and me of the congruencies between life in the Arabian and American deserts: the similarities in landscapes, cultures, and cuisines; the shared terms and bridged histories; and the historic characters that have happened to explore both regions in a state of raptured inquiry. I have tried to figure out both my own personal history and the history of the ancient Arab clan of my father: the Banu Nabhani, one of the ahl-Hadr tribes.

I have also wondered aloud whether desert creatures and desert cultures are inherently competitive for scarce resources in ways that inevitably lead to war. The answer I found to this question is far different from what I had originally anticipated, and it has actually offered me a modicum of hope. I have also come to understand that the Sonoran Desert borderlands where I have lived most of my life are full of place-names, plant names, and other lexical terms that came from Arabic and Berber into the Spanish of Andalusia. These terms later bled into Latin American Spanish before leaking into several Native American languages as well as into cowboy lingo. I now find traces of Arab words, foods, spices, and architectural and horticultural designs all around me in the American deserta.

And yet they are chimerical. I lived many years here without noticing any of them, and then one day a different light slanted in on them so that I could suddenly see them with clarity.

If, after reading this book, you occasionally see plants, irrigation canals, or Arabian horses differently, hear echoes of Arabic chants in music from the desert borderlands, or recognize the taste of certain Middle Eastern spices in your southwestern cuisine, I will be gratified that your own synaesthetic shift has begun. I will feel that my mission has been accomplished when and if Arabians and Americans fully appreciate their gifts to one another, as if they were brought together by a magi from a distant land.

Of course, many elements of American deserts are not shared with Arabian deserts and vice versa. So it is also my hope that you will savor the uniqueness of each and not gloss over their differences in discovering their similarities. Nevertheless, the human imagination is inherently fascinated by convergences, by parallels, by similes. May this comparative inquiry into Arabian and American desert landscapes, creatures, and cultures sharpen your eyes and your wits. Let it remind you that although each desert has its own distinctive character and characters, a living river of common heritage runs through them all.

I. Cultural, Ecological, and Culinary Connections Between Deserts

CHAPTER 1

Camel Whisperers

Desert Nomads Crossing Paths

AJO, ARIZONA, MAY seem at first like an unlikely place to uncover evidence of one of the great events linking the desert traditions of the Middle East with those of North America. It was once a prosperous copper-mining town, but since the mines went belly up, its multiethnic community has suffered from a number of economic insults. Although Ajo cannot support a great library with meticulously annotated historic archives and such, it has retained both its charm and a strong sense of its vernacular history through storytelling. Thanks to some rather remarkable women who decided to spend their last days in Ajo—Betty Melvin and Candelaria Orozco—we now know of an historic convergence between desert peoples and their animals that may seem as fortuitous as any event that has ever occurred on the face of the earth.

When I first met them, Candelaria was already more than a hundred years old; Betty was younger, but both were considered elders among the Hia c-eḍ O'odham, known to many as the nomadic Sand Papago of the Gran Desierto. In passing on this story, these women also helped me find something of my own cultural heritage transplanted some ten thousand miles to the desert borderlands of North America.

I first heard about this peculiar event from my friend, poet and linguist Ofelia Zepeda, who was interviewing Betty about the same time I was interviewing Candelaria. I occasionally brought Candelaria groceries and took her on field trips, for at that time she lived alone in a small clapboard shack, where she had a habit of storing desert roots and seeds under her bed. She and Betty were among the last surviving participants in their culture's ancient nomadic way of life, so Ofelia and I felt that they deserved a chance to tell their knowledge of the desert in ways that future generations might be able to hear.

One time, when Ofelia was working on her western O'odham oral

history project, Betty playfully ended their interview with a cryptic re-
minder of just how unique her own childhood had been. She had been
flipping through one of the little scrapbooks of pictures that Ofelia and I
used to elicit the ancient names for desert plants and animals in the Hia
c-eḍ O'odham native language, O'odham *ha-neokĭ*. After Betty had studied each picture and named each animal that she could recognize, she
closed the scrapbook and announced, "There is one other desert animal
that isn't in the pictures. It's the *cami:yo* that my people saw out in the
desert a long time ago."

I remember bursting out laughing when Ofelia first told me of Betty's
remark: "A camel in the desert? Not just in a zoo or a circus?"

But after I interviewed Candelaria, and Ofelia interviewed William
Merrill, another elder of their generation, we confirmed that the Hia c-eḍ
O'odham truly felt that camels had become members of their desert
bestiary. That is, they had genuinely incorporated stories of camels into
their oral traditions. From what we later pieced together, it must have
happened something like this.

A seminomadic group of O'odham were walking along through the
dunes and washes of the Gran Desierto when they began to notice tracks
made by some kind of rather large herbivore. The men finally stopped to
take a good look at the prints in the sand and determined that they were
quite fresh. Soon they began to argue among themselves, for one man
thought they were made by a bighorn sheep, but another thought they
belonged to an antelope, the Sonoran pronghorn. Finally, one of the
women present became impatient and blurted out: "I don't care what it is
exactly, as long as it is big, because I'm hungry. If the footprints are fresh,
and the animal is still nearby, let's just hunt it down and eat it."

That evening a small group of Sand Papago nomads savored camel
meat from one of the last dromedaries ever to roam the Sonoran Desert,
grilled over a campfire of ironwood and mesquite, thousands of miles
from the camel's original home.

Not long after I heard this story, I learned of another historic event
from about the same era. Some of my Nabhan kin have told me about an
incident that is said to have occurred between 1890 and 1915, around the
peak of Lebanese and Syrian immigration into the United States. One
unnamed ancestor of mine—young at the time and fresh off the boat—
somehow ended up in Saint Louis or Kansas City or Wichita (the place

always varying with the teller of the tale). According to all versions, this young Arab man began working as a menial laborer on a ditch-digging crew, something he found to be beneath his dignity. One morning, however, his fortune changed. While walking to work, he passed a zoo, where he saw a keeper struggling to move a camel from one enclosure to the next in order to clean the used enclosure.

The stubborn camel would not budge—that is, until my ancestor intervened. He began to speak to the camel and sing sweetly in Arabic, and when the camel heard these familiar sounds, he moved toward the edge of the enclosure. Tired from dealing with the uncooperative camel on his own, the zookeeper invited the young Arab immigrant into the enclosure. There my relative continued to romance the camel in Arabic and, taking its reins, casually but swiftly led it into the next enclosure. Impressed, the zookeeper talked to his boss about the miraculous event and hired the young immigrant as his camel-whispering helper right then and there, allowing him to leave behind his ditch-digging career for good!

This apocryphal story has the same ring sounded by so many tales told by the progeny of immigrants—fragments of urban folklore that are both untraceable through a living relative and otherwise unverifiable through other means. When I first heard of Candelaria's story of the O'odham eating camel meat, I subconsciously dismissed it, relegating it to the same category of tall tale as my family's lore. Later, however, I read a brief passage in an Arizona history about camels being let loose in the desert, and I was surprised to learn more recently from Greg Orfalea's fine book *The Arab Americans* that these camels were linked to one of the very first Syrian and Moslem immigrants to the United States.

Was it possible, I wondered, that the camel that Candelaria's O'odham kin consumed around the turn of the twentieth century was a descendant of the dromedaries brought to Arizona just before the Civil War?

I had never before imagined that I would become a private detective hot on the trail of a mysterious camel. And yet, by some strange fate, I began to gather clues to figure whether there might actually be a direct link between the first camels brought into the United States from the Middle East in 1856 and a desert feast on camel meat among some Sand Papago nomads as much as a half-century later.

After I had finally done some sleuthing, I was struck by the very weirdness of the particular characters and creatures that played key roles in this story, and I became convinced that the savoring of camel flesh by some Sand Papago nomads was perhaps *the least-improbable* element of the entire tale. An altogether astonishing sequence of events was triggered in American *deserta* by the appearance of an enigmatic man variously known as Filippou Teodora, Philip Tedro, Felipe Teatro, Hadji Ali, and Hi Jolly. He appears to be the first Moslem from the Middle East to arrive on the North American continent, and he came in the company of camels. By pulling off the first and only dromedary drive to cross the entire desert Southwest, Hadji Ali became one the most peculiar heroes that Western history buffs have ever celebrated.

If I have pieced together the clues correctly, the man who became the first camel drover in the American deserta was likely to have been called Filippou Teodora following his birth in 1828. In Greek, *teodors* and *teodora* mean "a gift of God," and *filippou* means "the lover of horses." And yet it turned out to be camels—not horses—that Philip came to love, in lands that most visitors consider to be *god forsaken*. Philip's early family history has been obscured, as if some dust storm swept it away. His father was likely the Syrian in the family, for his mother was reputed to be a Greek who was captured by Arabs when she was young, only to take another Arab, likely a Syrian, as a partner when she was older. They resided not in Greece or Syria, but in Smyrna, Turkey, a port town now known as Izmir. Although Filippou Teodora spelled his surname *Tedro* when he became a naturalized citizen of the United States some three decades later, the surname "Teodora" remains common in Izmir today. Another of the first camel drovers to come to the United States was his cousin "Mico," who consistently gave his full name as Mimico Teodora from the year 1855, when first seen at the Old Caravan Bridge in Smyrna, until around 1896, when he disappeared from Southwest history, leaving Mico Creek in Kerr County, Texas, as his only legacy. Filippou Teodora was something of a chimerical changeling, shifting cultures, countries, continents, citizenry, and occupations at will, but his cousin was less so, which has helped me tether Filippou to his rather obscure roots.

The trail tracing Filippou Teodora's early life in the Middle East has grown cold over the past century, leaving only three other facts for us to ruminate upon. Before he reached twenty-five years of age, he converted from the Orthodox Christian faith to Islam, making a hajj (*hadj*), or sacred pilgrimage, to Mecca. To commemorate the significance of this hadj to his very identity, he assumed the name "Hadji Ali." Then, presumably just after his conversion, he served with the French Foreign Legion in Algiers in the capacity of an appraiser for their purchasing commission. Perhaps it was during this service that he became adept in the military use, care, and feeding of camels. It appears that he gained some rudimentary knowledge of French and perhaps some other Western languages at this time as well.

After service in Algiers, Hadji Ali made it back to Constantinople and then to Smyrna by 1855, just in time to meet an American entrepreneur named Gwin Harris Heap, who had come in advance of the USS *Supply*, looking for both camels and their drovers to participate in a little experiment back in the deserts of North America. Heap apparently took an immediate liking to Philip and Mico, for he dispatched them to the Turkish interior to purchase additional camels. Soon after Philip and Mico returned with both Bactrians and dromedaries, they left the Middle East for the desert Southwest.

It appears that Philip was the first Moslem of Syrian ancestry to make a home and family in the United States. Along the way, he would become inextricably entangled in efforts by the U.S. military to secure the entire Southwest from its Mexican adversaries, by Jefferson Davis to connect the Deep South with the wealth of California, by Sonorans to escape corrupt politicians in Mexico, and by nomadic O'odham hunter-gatherers to feed themselves in the desert. Perhaps to Philip's surprise, there were men and women in America who apparently felt they needed camels and camel drovers to help accomplish all of these feats.

All of this begs the simple question: What on earth motivated Americans like Heap—at that particular moment in history—to travel to the Middle East seeking camels? The simplest answer is that as the U.S. government expanded the territory it controlled, a transportation crisis arose that some people thought camels could solve. It was the era just prior to the completion of the transcontinental railroad, and neither horses nor mules could carry loads large enough to supply all needed provisions to America's remote outposts. The crisis was precipitated when the United States took control of some 529,000 square miles of dry lands between Louisiana and the Pacific Ocean. The government suddenly needed more efficient means to supply the outposts it established to guard and monitor these lands. Because much of this area was then known as the "Great American Desert" and was perceived to be a virtually uninhabitable wasteland, some individuals hoped that camels would serve as a quick technological fix. Consider this crisis the nineteenth-century equivalent of gasoline prices skyrocketing at the start of the twenty-first century, and you can imagine that camels looked as good as hybrid cars look today.

The Quartermaster Department of the U.S. government was finding it terribly difficult to deliver much-needed supplies to the forts established on the southwestern lands that had been taken as possessions between 1848 and 1853, after the dust had settled from the Mexican-American War and the Gadsden Purchase. The remoteness of the strategic forts scattered across the territory meant that the transportation budget for their periodic provisioning soared.

In fact, the Quartermaster Department's budget for supplying military forts in the Southwest suddenly eclipsed the pre–Civil War budget for the entire U.S. Army left in the East. Camels were advanced as just the ticket for dealing with this costly transportation problem until freight cars loaded onto a transcontinental railroad could offer a more permanent solution.

This story works well if we assume that camels were specifically proposed for introduction by someone attempting to solve the transportation problem for the entire Great American Desert. It is not surprising that some historians credit Jefferson Davis for finessing the translocation of the first camels into the United States. Davis, appointed as the secretary of war by President Franklin Pierce, was the one who ultimately had to go to Congress to deal with the needs of all those new military outposts in the desert.

Jefferson Davis had another, longer-term goal in mind as well, however, for he had also begun to plan a southerly route for the transcontinental railroad—a route he hoped could be built before the Yankees completed one between Chicago and northern California. Indeed, Davis hoped that the use of camels would hasten the process of charting a specific route through the dry, rugged lands stretching between New Orleans and San Diego. If he could quickly get a railroad line built on this route that could access the astonishing amount of wealth being generated in the California gold rush, the South might be able to repel the North's demands for abolition of slavery—and perhaps with this wealth even establish a confederation strong enough to break away altogether from the North.

Although Jefferson Davis can be credited with implementing the proposal of purchasing camels for use in the Great American Desert, he was not its genius. The original vision and initial lobbying came from a man with no direct experience in that desert or in any other, no role in the formative stages of a transcontinental railroad, and no inkling of how a war with Mexico or a civil war might later affect the United States. In fact, this man began dreaming of camels more than a decade before these wars came upon the American horizon, when he was stationed not in a desert, but in the humid backwaters of Florida during the Seminole Wars of the mid-1830s.

His name was George H. Crosman, and he was a second lieutenant in the U.S. Army who served as quartermaster for troops in the Deep South. In 1836, he first pitched the idea to some bureaucrats in Washington, D.C., with the help of his friend E. F. Miller of Ipswich, Massachusetts, who later recorded their logic in this manner:

> For strength in carrying burdens, for patient endurance of labor, and privation of food, water & rest, and in some respects for speed also, the [Bactrian] camel and the dromedary (as the Arabian camel is called) are unrivaled among animals. The ordinary loads for camels are from seven to nine to ten hundred pounds each, and with these they can travel from thirty to forty miles per day, for many days in succession. They will go without water, and with but little food, for six or eight days, or it is said even longer. Their feet are alike well suited for traversing grassy or sandy plains, or rough, rocky & hilly paths, and they require no shoeing.

Of course, these rather attractive attributes could be made manifest only if there were a seasoned camel whisperer to suppress the beasts' innate tendency toward orneriness. Crosman soon realized he needed both camels and experienced camel drovers.

Crosman somehow got the ear of another quartermaster, Henry C. Wayne, who first pitched the idea to Jefferson Davis when Davis was still senator from Mississippi in 1848. Chair of the Senate Committee on Military Affairs, Davis began to advocate for the experimental introduction of camels just as the Gadsden Purchase of the Great American Desert was taking place. But it was not until Davis became appointed secretary of war that the idea got some legs. In a December 1853 report, he encouraged President Pierce to go to Congress for at least thirty thousand dollars in funds to import camels to solve the impending transportation crisis: "For military purposes, for expresses, and for reconnaissance, it is believed, the dromedary would supply a want now seriously felt in our service; and for transportation with troops rapidly moving across the country, the camel, it is believed, would remove an obstacle which now serves to greatly diminish the value and efficiency of our troops on the western frontier."

Fortunately for Davis, there was someone outside the government at the time who began to lobby just as hard for camel importation. This person was Philip and Mico Teodora's agent for their life in the New World, an indefatigable promoter and romanticist named Gwin Harris Heap. Enraptured by a travelogue that praised the utility of camels—Abbe Huc's *Travels in Tartary, Tibet, and China, during the Years 1844, 1845, and 1846*—Heap passed copies of it around to senators, congressmen, and a relative of his, Edward Fitzgerald Beale, who was then the superintendent of Indian Affairs in the western territory. Beale was at first unimpressed by Heap's propaganda regarding camels, but upon reading Huc's engaging account of these animals, he warmed up to the idea.

When the congressional appropriation for camels finally passed through both the House and the Senate on March 3, 1855, Beale immediately heard about it from Heap and got one of their other relatives to apply for the command of the expedition to the Middle East. That relative, a navy lieutenant later immortalized as Admiral David Dixon Porter, did indeed apply, but ended up sharing the command with Major Wayne, Crosman's colleague who had first pitched the proposal to Davis. Porter would take charge of the USS *Supply*, a sort of Noah's Ark, and Major Wayne would take care of the business transactions and livestock-management issues. By the summer of 1855, Wayne, Porter, and Heap were off to the Mediterranean to study, purchase, and transport camels, and by the next winter they had enlisted the help of Hadji Ali in this peculiar endeavor.

Without implying that either Major Wayne or Lieutenant Porter was suddenly out of his league, let us just concede that they suffered a number of false starts before they met up with Hadji Ali. The two men joined together in Italy, but the camels seen there in the custody of the grand duke of Tuscany were overworked and so poorly cared for that none was worth purchasing. They then sailed to Tunis, where local merchants, probably noticing how anxious they were to begin their purchases, sold Major Wayne a "lemon," a rather unremarkable two-humped Bactrian specimen. The bey of Tunisia then offered them a pair of one-humped Arabian camels in exceptional condition as a gift to demonstrate his goodwill toward the president of the United States. The USS *Supply* sailed on to Malta and then to Turkey and Egypt, where Wayne and Porter ran into trouble with a pasha's prohibition against exporting live-stock without permits. After numerous tedious negotiations, they left Egypt with six additional dromedaries and some ne'er-do-well Egyptian caretakers, but the latter suffered so much from seasickness that they left the expedition before it arrived in Texas.

Gwin Heap had already gone on to Constantinople and then to Smyrna, where he met Porter and Wayne on January 30, 1856, with some good news. He not only had obtained access to four Arabian males and fifteen females, but had found a Bactrian-Arabian cross and another two-humped Bactrian. Heap had also lined up a bunch of Greeks and Turks to take the place of the Egyptians, but most of them turned out to be city slickers from Constantinople who had feigned experience with camels in order to get a free ride to the United States. They proved to be hardly more helpful than the seasick Egyptians, but five of them made it the entire way to Texas before they too disappeared.

Fortunately, Heap, Porter, and Wayne were able to recruit three men in the Aegean port of Smyrna who saved the day. The one they called "Greek George"—Yiorgos Caralambo—later ran camels along the Butter-field Stage route, eventually changed his name to George Allen, and ran a stable for a retired army man named Hancocks at Rancho la Brea near Los Angeles, the now-famous site where bones of extinct species of pre-historic camels were later found. The other two, whom we assume to be kin, were the Teodoras—Mico and Filippou—the latter having recently changed his name to Hadji Ali. They appeared to be the only souls on board the USS *Supply* who truly knew how to handle camels, and they helped Porter prepare his ark for the animals' safe handling during the long voyage. Heap, in particular, was impressed by the one Teodora named Philip: "This swarthy little Arab with sharp dark eyes proved so helpful in teaching [us] about camels that [we] made him one of seven

. . . to return with them to America." On February 15, 1856, they set sail with thirty-three camels standing side to side on the flat bottom of the ship, with their backs just clearing the deck. Hadji Ali and his cohorts left the Middle East for America, never to return.

We have no idea what the camel caretakers ate during the three months of transcontinental voyage, but we do know what the camels ate and when. Each animal was given a gallon of oats or mixed oats and peas at three o'clock every afternoon, and their hay racks in front of them were filled with as much as ten pounds of dried grass. Each animal was also allowed three gallons of water per day to wash down their feed. When gales rose up and the ship was tossed around by the swales, the camels went down on their knees and haunches, and ate kneeling, as if taking communion. A few of the males nibbled whitewash off the beams and deck during the rutting season, but survived even that. One female died while calving; six calves were born, but four of them died along the way. It was the longest trip ever taken by any camel and the farthest that their drover, Hadji Ali, had strayed from home.

Thirty-four camels were on board when the USS *Supply* reached the other side of the Atlantic at Kingston-town on the coast of Jamaica. After a short break for the sailors in Kingston, the ship continued its journey and arrived on the Texas coast in the spring of 1856. After several aborted attempts were made at landing the USS *Supply*'s heralded load, the camels were transferred to the more maneuverable *Fashion*. They were finally brought to land at Powder Horn, Texas, three miles south of Indianola, on May 14, 1856, roughly 8,500 miles from where they had begun their journey. Thanks to Major Wayne, we have a fleeting glimpse of the spectacle made by the first camels to set foot on American soil in some eight to ten thousand years: "On being landed, and feeling once again the solid earth beneath them, they became excited to an uncontrollable degree, rearing, kicking, crying out, breaking halters, tearing up pickets, and by other fantastic tricks demonstrating their enjoyment of the liberty of the soil."

It took probably all Hadji Ali's patience and skill to drive them the three miles along the floodplain upriver to Indianola and herd them into a stable specially erected for them by the quartermaster. At last, the camels and their drovers reported for duty with the U.S. Army.

As was typical in the Great American Desert, though, things did not exactly proceed as planned. Some problems arose with the military contract negotiated with the foreign drovers, for it specified that the men, once the camels arrived in Texas, were obligated to work only six months. Then, if they chose not to stay, they would be granted a bonus, discharged, and given a free berth on the next navy ship bound for their home. Two of the Turks saw little of value in the backwaters of Texas that could keep them there and immediately opted to leave. Most of the Greek city slickers from Constantinople stayed on for a while, but became frustrated and refused to work when their pay did not arrive as expected. One of the Syrian Arabs who went AWOL was named Elias; years later, when he settled in Sonora, he was known by the nickname "El Turco," married a Yaqui woman, and fathered the future president of Mexico, Plutarco Elias Calles. With most of their friends fleeing, it fell to Hadji Ali, Mico Teodora, and Yiorgos Caralambo to muster some order out of the herd. Whatever these young men had initially lacked in camel-driving skills, they made up for with their tenacity and perspicacity.

The camels and the military bureaucracy were not the only problems with which the immigrants had to contend, though. To their dismay, the Texas cowboys milling about Indianola began to treat both the camels and their drovers with considerable scorn. The foot soldiers enlisted by the Quartermaster Department refused to have anything to do with the ungainly and rather ugly animals. Finally, Major Wayne caught wind of this derision and arranged a spectacle of his own. He brought a camel in front of a crowd of hecklers and slowly loaded him down with some two thousand pounds of supplies. As Wayne later recalled, "The gaping crowd gave noisy expression to their astonishment and indignation, and gentlemen who had never been to camel land were 'willing to bet that the critter couldn't git up under the heft of that.' But when the camel arose, without strain, and quietly walked away with his four bales . . . there was a sudden change in public sentiment, most flattering to the outlandish brute and encouraging to his military sponsors."

By the time the first class of camels became acclimatized and were trained, Hadji Ali arrived in Indianola with a second batch of camels. They, too, needed training and acclimation, and it was Hadji Ali who quickly whipped them into shape. As one observer witnessed the scene at the training grounds,

There was only one man who appeared to have any influence with the bewildered beasts. Slender built and in his middle 30's, the assembled Texans saw him as a rather attractive chap with a flashing, white-toothed smile, black eyes and curly hair. Moving quietly among the restless animals, he spoke to them in a soft, foreign tongue, reassuring them, placating them, as a mother might speak to a fretful child. Gradually it became apparent to the crowd that this dark-skinned fellow, alone, was bringing order out of chaos.

The camels were now broken, but it was a motley, multilingual crew of immigrants and enlisted men that drove the animals from the south coast of Texas all the way to Big Bend in western Texas. The man now known as Hi Jolly had to teach the others how to read the camels' body language: when their humps were firm and elevated, the beasts were well nourished and working at capacity; but when the humps sagged, they were overtaxed and stressed. This first cross-country trek did indeed overburden some of the beasts, so the men rested them for a while at Fort Davis, where Heap's kinsman, Ned Beale, reappeared on the scene to take command. Beale had gone from the petty job of Indian commissioner presiding over the relations with several tribes to become the leader of one of the most widely heralded transportation experiments in Western history.

Beale gained control of the troops around the time they arrived in Albuquerque, where he immediately realized that camel drovers, alcohol, and bordellos do not make a very pretty combination. He was particularly critical of the Moslems who got drunk, for he assumed they would abstain from alcohol. At the same time, however, he singled out Hadji Ali as being the most reliable among his rowdy camel corps.

He directed the caravan away from any more party towns, sending it off toward El Morro near Zuni, then into the Little Colorado River drainage, where they crossed the Painted Desert. They then rose in elevation until they skirted the slopes of the San Francisco Peaks near Flagstaff. From there, they edged the south rim of the Grand Canyon until they passed near Peach Springs, where the Hualapai Indians had congregated. After Peach Springs, they went over to Kingman and down through the Mojave Desert along Triton Wash, to the banks of the Colorado River near Needles, a Mohave Indian camp. There, the sight of the camels caused quite a stir among the Mohave Indians, who began to wail in their rudimentary

English, *"God damn my soul eyes! How de do! How de do!"* The Mohave later elaborated the form of a camel as an intaglio in the desert pavement near Needles to commemorate the event.

California was now in sight, but Hi Jolly still had some work to do to convince the camels that it was worth crossing a river to get to that promised land. When the lead camel was faced with deep water immediately before him, it would not budge and bellowed like it was bound to die. So Hi Jolly tied five of the calmer camels together, with one of his favorites in the lead—most likely Sa'id, a ten-foot-long, seven-and-a-half-foot-tall dromedary. Whispering sweet nothings in that camel's ear, Hi Jolly cajoled him to the far shore. Another group of camels followed, and then another, until all had successfully forded the Río Colorado—that is, all of the *camels*. Ned Beale's soldiers were having a far tougher time getting their horses and mules to cross to safety. By the time the sun went down on October 17, 1857, two horses and ten mules had drowned. Watching all the turmoil, the Mohave offered the troops their cantaloupes and watermelons, perhaps to console them for the loss of their mounts.

Having crossed the last obstacle of their journey, the group of men, horses, mules, and camels arrived at Fort Tejon, California, still bearing loads of six to eight hundred pounds, in November 1857. Although the men and the camels' feet were worse for wear, Commander Ned Beale stood amazed: "The harder the test they [the camels] are put to, the more fully they seem to justify all that can be said of them. They pack water for days under a hot sun and never get a drop; they pack heavy burdens of corn and oats for months and never get a grain; and on the bitter greasewood [creosote] and other worthless shrubs, they not only persist, but keep fat."

It soon became glaringly apparent, though, that few Americans were initially as impressed by the camels' performance as Beale was. The army regulars who accompanied the camels from Texas to California never bonded with the camels. They disparaged their smell, their habit of spitting, their gait, their temperament, and their lack of utility when not shouldering heavy loads. In short, camels weren't made for cowboys.

From another perspective, the performance of a few camels way out west did not matter all that much in the eyes of eastern military leaders on the verge of a civil war. Jefferson Davis was at the heart and center of the growing political schism in the East and was replaced by John B. Floyd as secretary of war in 1857. Distracted, Floyd failed in his attempts to get two further congressional appropriations for the camel experiment. The Quartermaster Department found funds to support the camels and their drovers through 1860. The department's official camel experiment was being brought to a close, though for a while the camels remained the property of the military. The remaining drovers, including Hi Jolly, assumed naïvely that they were awaiting another assignment in their permanent employment package.

At first, they did receive a few minor assignments. From 1857 to 1860, Beale occasionally employed Hi Jolly and Greek George to run camel caravans from the port of Los Angeles to supply Fort Tejon. They also made a run with the camels up to Lake Tahoe in the service of Sylvester Mowry, who later became one of the Arizona Territory's most prominent statesmen. By the end of 1857, Hi Jolly and Greek George had spent enough time in government service to become naturalized citizens of the United States, which encouraged Hi Jolly to begin deliveries across the desert by mule on behalf of the U.S. Postal Service, gaining him a reputation as the bringer of "jackass mail." For a while, it seemed as though the camel drovers had simply been reassigned to more localized tasks.

However, trouble was brewing. The man Floyd had appointed to lead the army in the Southwest hated camels with a ferocity that astonished his peers. According to historian Diane Yancey, Major General David E. Twiggs "was outraged when he discovered a herd of camels under his command." In his mind, horses and mules were the only mounts suitable for his cavalry. And Floyd, with a civil war bearing down upon him, had more immediate concerns than to defend the camels against one of his major generals. As the union faltered in the early 1860s, any tentative plans for using the camels were abandoned, their advocates scattered by the winds of war.

Thus stranded in the Mojave Desert of southern California, Hi Jolly and Greek George continued their care of the camels right up until the time when the federal government ordered the animals to be liquidated. The first batch of thirty-four was auctioned at Benicia, and others went to circuses, cotton plantations, and mines. But few of their new owners knew how to whisper to the reluctant beasts, to cajole and coax them, to remind them of their stature and strength.

Within weeks, several of the auctioned camels escaped from the servitude of those illiterate in the ways of the dromedary. They quickly went feral, surviving by their wits in a desert somewhat different from their own. Hi Jolly and Greek George soon went after these animals and rescued others from their disgruntled owners, thereafter keeping them without official sanction at Fort Yuma on the Arizona-California border until 1866. After the Civil War, when army bureaucrats regained some focus, it dawned on them that they were still subsidizing the care and feeding of camels that were no longer officially theirs to keep. For a second time, they released from duty both the remaining camels and their drovers. Greek George got the message and headed westward to work for Hancocks at Rancho la Brea. Hi Jolly kept most of the camels and occasionally used them to run supplies from Yuma to mines near Wellton and Gila Bend, all in Arizona, and into northern Sonora.

After several years of serving as a scout at Fort McDowell in the army campaign against the Apaches, Hi Jolly established a more regular camel freight route from Yuma to Tucson. There he met a Sonoran woman named Gertrudis Serna, whom he married in 1880. She was kin to an activist from Puerto Libertad named Francisco Serna, who had led an insurrection against a corrupt Sonoran governor Ignacio Pesquiera. The governor had prevailed with the help of the Mexican National Guard, and many *sernistas* fled to Tucson to escape his wrath. Taking refuge in the Old Pueblo (Tucson), Gertrudis and Hi Jolly—who now went by the name Philip Tedro or, rarely, Felipe Teatro—tried to make a stable home together. They had two daughters, Amelia and Herminia, who grew up in Tucson. For a while, Philip worked as a saddle maker, trying to adapt to a more sedentary life.

It soon became all too clear, however, that Philip was constitutionally unfit for living in a fixed abode. He, like his camels, could not stay very long in one place before being overtaken by the urge to roam once more. He began prospecting again, this time with mules as his allies because he had reluctantly released the camels about the time his girls were born. He searched for ore near Washington Camp in southern Arizona, then strayed farther afield, working for the San Augustín Mining Company in northern Sonora.

Philip began living away from his wife and daughters for longer and longer periods of time, until Gertrudis gave up waiting for his support. Fleeing from her complaints, he roughed out another abode for himself at Tyson's Well, Arizona, near the present-day town of Quartzite. There, he corralled more feral camels and befriended everyone from Indian farmers to lawyers, politicians, and drunk prospectors. Although his neighbors occasionally cursed his camels for scaring their horses, Philip became somewhat of a celebrity around Quartzite. A mining engineer named Joseph Obermuller recalled that Philip had become a famed storyteller, amazing all listeners with tales of how he had tracked another wild bunch of nomads, the Western Apaches: "Mr. Tedro was well liked by those that knew him. He would tell many interesting incidents that happened while in the services of the Army during Indian fighting and especially the fight against Geronimo."

Whenever one of Philip's admirers spotted a feral camel roaming in the desert, they would fetch him to track it down and tame it. Tom Childs Jr., while living among his nomadic Sand Papago (O'odham) in-laws about the time that Candelaria Orozco was born, found Philip in hot pursuit of camels near Ajo: "Old man Hi Jolly, the Arab that helped bring camels into this country, came to my place at Ajo in 1888 or '89 to try to catch some to prospect with. Some of these camels reached as far down as the Gulf of California, but they were easy prey for the Papagos. They were all gentle and easy to get up to. Hi Jolly lived at my home in Ajo and used to tell me stories of his travels with camels . . . from El Paso to San Diego, and some of the races he won [with the camels] against horses."

It is the oddest of coincidences that an Arab nomad from the Middle East had found his way some ten thousand miles to live among the last indigenous nomads remaining in the United States. We will never know what the Sand Papago thought of Hi Jolly or he of them, but they shared a natural affinity for more than the mere pursuit of camels. Hi Jolly never caught up with the camels that Childs had learned of from the Sand Papago; perhaps they were the very ones that Candelaria Orozco's kin later ate.

Whether these camels were remnants of the original herd no one knows, for two other introductions of camels to the desert occurred while Hi Jolly was still alive. More Bactrian herds had been introduced through San Francisco in the 1860s and had made their way into the Great American Desert, and Hi Jolly himself had unloaded fifty dromedaries from a steamer that reached Yuma in 1872. The remnants of at least four camel introductions coalesced to form a wild breeding population of at least one hundred sexually mature animals in the Gila River valley. They adapted to a diet of Sonoran Desert cacti and mesquite, so much so that they exhibited both high reproductive rates and considerable vigor.

Although the camels remained vigorous, Hi Jolly himself was in decline. The rigors of a solitary life in the desert had finally broken him down. In 1898, his estranged wife, Gertrudis, found that he had been hospitalized in Tucson. She went to visit him, but would not bring their daughters to St. Mary's Hospital to see him and refused to take him in. On another occasion, his friend Obermuller found Hi Jolly so sick that he picked him up and paid his way to a Phoenix hospital on a stagecoach that went up the Gila. Then in 1901, Hi Jolly again landed in a ward at St. Mary's. He returned to the desert as soon as he was able and, according to Obermuller, finally decided to enlist the help of his friends in order to obtain some health care and financial aid through the military. "It was not until the ravages of time and toil broke upon him that Hi Jolly undertook to get a pension from the U.S. government. He sought no charity."

He had first talked of putting his papers in order some two decades earlier, when he had realized he was no longer in the service of an army that he believed had offered him the kind of lifetime commitment that Turks back at home expect from their sultans. In an interview he gave to the *Arizona Gazette* in 1885, he maintained that "[b]y terms of the contract, [he] was to receive employment as long as he chose to remain in the United States, and transportation and commutation of rations whenever he desired to return to his native land."

In a statement written for him in 1901, Hi Jolly pleaded with the Arizona Territory's delegate to Congress, Marcus A. Smith, to secure him a pension of fifteen dollars a month. His pension application noted that "thirty years of frontier service have so undermined my constitution and broken me down that now in my old age, I find myself no longer able to gain a livelihood." He attached to the application a letter written on his behalf in 1899 by Colonel George B. Sanford, with whom he had served at Fort McDowell up until Geronimo's surrender in 1886, when his last paying job for the military came to an end: "It was always understood that the government has had few more faithful servants in the last half century."

Others—including generals, senators, and the governor of the Arizona Territory, N. O. Smith—rallied to Hi Jolly's defense and affirmed the justice of the claim he submitted. Despite all this support, however, the federal commissioner of pensions ruled against him, informing Delegate Marcus Smith that the army had retained no record of any written agreement with Hi Jolly and could not corroborate what he had been told through a translator. Smith wrote to Hi Jolly that the decision could not be overturned except if Congress passed a special act on his behalf. He discouraged Hi Jolly's friends from pursuing such a measure because the House committee overseeing such initiatives had been averse to enacting special legislation since the Civil War. Besides, Marcus Smith asserted, "Hi Jolly was not a citizen of the United States. He had suffered no injury in the Apache war. No written contract was on record."

Hi Jolly, having believed that he had been a naturalized citizen of the United States since 1857, belatedly realized that as an Arab immigrant he had never really gained all the rights of citizens born in the United States. His health and his hope continued to decline. On December 16, 1902, while trying to recuperate his strength, he died somewhere along an old desert road between Wickenberg, Arizona, and the Colorado River. Sixty-four years old at the time, he left only three silver coins worth forty cents, a pack of tobacco, and his line shack at Tyson's Well.

Curiously, the friends who were the last to see Hi Jolly alive claimed that he had told them he'd be out on the Colorado River road looking for camels. One of those friends was a Texan named Jimmy Walker, who had met Hi Jolly when he was still back in Indianola with his cousin Mico. Walker claims to have been talking with some local cowhands in a cantina in Quartzite about a recent camel sighting when Hi Jolly overheard him. According to the Texan, the old Arab blurted out, "Boys, where's that camel?" Once he heard their report, he pulled his hat brim down to shade his eyes and walked out of the cantina in the direction that the cowpokes gave him.

The next day Hi Jolly passed from a life on earth into the world of myth. As Walker recounted the story to Chris Emmett some three decades later, in 1932, the cowboys were out hunting for cattle the next day when they spotted somebody—or someone's body—slumped on the ground, partially covered by drifting sands from the previous night's desert winds. Hi Jolly was in that drift, Walker said, having died with his arms around the neck of a long-lost camel, which had also perished in the dark of a sand storm.

The last camel in captivity from the original 1856 herd died in 1934 in the Garfield Zoo of Los Angeles at an estimated age of eighty, having lived for longer than most camels live in the Sahara or the Levant. Its ashes were later put in a vault within a stone pyramid at Hi Jolly's last camp, erected in Quartzite by the Arizona Highway Department. At a ceremony two years after the camel's death, Miss Elizabeth Toohey, Arizona's state historian, decried the U.S. government's treatment not only of the camels, but of Hi Jolly, their most acclaimed drover. She mourned that "we left him alone to know the sting of poverty and the humiliation of a man who had outlived his usefulness."

But camels had not yet outlived their usefulness in the Great American Desert. Several still roamed there even as Miss Toohey spoke. More than a hundred had been rounded up by Mohave Indians over the years to be sent to circuses in the East. The final camel found in the wilds of Arizona was reputedly captured in 1946, well after Candelaria's nomadic kin had feasted on camel meat. Remarkably, the most recently reported glimpse of a feral camel in the North America deserta occurred in Baja California in 1956. If camels seldom live past fifty years in age, the creature sighted must have been a grandchild of the camels brought over to the Great American Desert by Hadji Ali and his camel friends.

The official use of camels as beasts of burden by the U.S. Army lasted scarcely a decade, and few desert dwellers other than Candelaria and her kin ever ate camel meat. Although camels failed to take on the economic importance in the Great American Desert that they have had for millennia in the Middle East, they have assumed mythic importance nonetheless, becoming part of Americana in legend, festival, song, and icon.

A camel known as the Red Ghost trampled an Arizona woman in 1883, then temporarily vanished from sight. And yet it continues to reappear in the desert every once in a while, roaming through Western folktales to this day. Although the camels still wander like phantoms, the memory of Hi Jolly has been cemented into a mass of kitsch. Quartzite, Arizona, celebrates an annual festival called Hi Jolly Daze, one of the few grassroots events in America commemorating a Moslem immigrant from the Middle East. The town has been home to the Hi Jolly Rock Shop, the Hi Ali Motel, and the Hi Jolly Liquor Store, though not all of the customers who frequent these places realize whom their business is honoring. The "Ballad of Hi Jolly" is still sung around campfires in the West, and at least two movies have Western heroes crudely based on Hadji Ali and Yiorgos "Greek George" Caralambo.

The legacy of a Moslem who went by a half-dozen names during his lifetime is an odd one. He was born as Philip, the lover of horses. His cultural heritage was both Syrian and Greek, but he became a camel whisperer in Turkey, Algiers, Arizona, California, Nevada, and Sonora. He married a Sonoran, but then abandoned her and their daughters to become a well-loved nomad of the desert borderlands. He walked to Mecca on his own two feet, but he crossed the Colorado River on a camel named Sa'id. The only words of his ever recorded for posterity were spoken to his burro, not to another human. They were scribbled on the back of a photograph taken of him and his burro, Johnny, by a Mr. Ross of Phoenix in 1896, when Ross visited Hadji Ali out at Agua Caliente Spring, not far from Tyson's Well. After posing for a couple of Mr. Ross's photos, Hadji Ali turned to his burro and quipped: "You're getting dam stylish just for getting your picture took, Johnny."

Hadji Ali's love of camels has been remembered more than his love for horses or burros like Johnny, perhaps simply because those of us who love deserts are invariably curious about camels—we love to imagine them, love to draw them, and love to give them praise. Perhaps it is because we love the exotic and quixotic, particularly when they show up suddenly in our midst and especially if they echo a remote and rarified desert we have wandered into during our deepest dreams.

CHAPTER 2

¿Eres Paisano?

The Culinary Influences of Arabia and al-Andalus in the U.S. Southwest and Mexico

WHEN YOU HAVE BEEN traveling all day through the desolate reaches of the Zona de Silencio in the Chihuahuan Desert, enduring temperatures that make the road before you shimmer like a red-hot coal in a campfire, you are more likely than not inclined to veer off the road at the first sighting of a cantina that has a sign above it announcing "El Oasis."

"I do not give one rat's ass what kind of food they have," said my fellow traveler, a cactomaniac named Peggy, "as long as they have something exceedingly cold to drink."

I took her at her word. By the time I got out of the Jeep and headed into the small café on the edge of La Laguna, the irrigated basin surrounding Torreón, Coahuila, Peggy was already sitting at a table, reading the menu, and having second thoughts.

"This really chafes my hiney," she said, sighing. "I've been eating Mexican food in Texican restaurants for years, and never have I seen *any* of the stuff that's on this menu. What the hell is *jocoque?*"

I wiped my eyes and tried to look at the menu before me, but I couldn't yet read it. In the fifty yards I had covered between the Jeep and the front door of the air-conditioned El Oasis, the heat had blurred my vision and burned my eyes with salt. As I adjusted to the dim light and cool air of the Coahuilan café, I realized that Peggy was right; the menu was filled with mention of dishes unavailable at most Tex-Mex drive-ins and bars. Nonetheless, these dishes formed a peculiar part of northern Mexican cuisine and had deep roots in desert dietaries as well.

"Jocoque, Peggy dearest, is a cool, soothing yogurtlike drink that's an old tradition in these parts." I'd first had it at the nearby home of José Muruaga Martínez, a Mexican agronomist of Andalusian and Moorish descent, who traveled with me for a month through the desert borderlands as we collected seeds and roots of wild beans. His mother had brought some jocoque to us in tall, frosted glasses when we arrived at their home on the other side of the Laguna basin, closer to Gomez Palacios, Durango.

"Unless you want to start a tab for margaritas at high noon," I suggested to her, "jocoque would be a good way to quench your thirst."

"That sounds fine," she said, "but what the heck is all this other stuff?"

"Well, *hojas de vid* are stuffed grape leaves; *berenjena asada* is grilled eggplant; *jumus bi-tajin con limón* is mashed chickpeas with sesame paste and lime juice, *eftoyer* must be the triangular *fatayer* pies, and *quebbe* is . . . well, it must be kibbe—you know, ground lamb with onions, bulgur wheat, and piñon nuts."

"No, I don't know what kibbe is. What do you suggest that I eat? I just want to cool down."

"Well, Peg, I'd suggest the jocoque, grape leaves, and jumus bi-tajin for starters."

Just then I heard some chuckling coming from behind me. I looked over my shoulder, and there stood a man with curly, shiny black hair, a dapper mustache, a beaked nose, and baggy eyes. He looked at me for a moment and listened as I rattled off more options for Peggy to consider for our *mezze*.

The chef then put his hand on my shoulder and warmly greeted me. "Mahlhabba! ¿Eres paisano?"

I was stunned for a moment. I understood the Arab greeting *mahlhabba*, but what about his asking me if I were a *paisano*. A peasant? A tiller of the soil? A roadrunner? Then it came to me: *a countryman. Are you a fellow countryman?*

So far from the motherland, a chance encounter with distant kin . . .

While Peggy ordered for both of us—simply pointing to items on the menu—I sat in silence, smiling at a long-lost cousin, trying to hold back my tears. They were tears of joy, tears of reunion. Wherever there is Arabic food on a desert table, there is *homecoming*.

Jocoque, hummus, grape leaves, and lamb kibbe are not the only Arabian flavors that have made it to the American deserts. Wherever there is an oasislike agricultural area on either side of the U.S.–Mexico border, there are groves of dates, figs, olives, apricots, grape vines, pomegranates, and citrus, just as there are on the Arabian Peninsula. In garden patches within and among these groves, lentils, peas, favas, and chickpeas are grown in rows, with okra, eggplants, cucumbers, melons, garlic, and Egyptian multiplier onions forming patches around them. Just as in the Middle East, goats and sheep abound in the semiarid steppe found in the rugged uplands surrounding these oases. Their salty cheeses add flavor and texture to many Middle Eastern–influenced meals. Although some spices and nuts must still be imported to the New World, Arab immigrants to northern Mexico and the U.S. Southwest have found analogous pine nuts, oreganos, mints, and sumac berries to substitute into their recipes.

Even some prepared foods assumed to be authentically American dishes—from *mole poblanos* to *chiles en nogadas* and *huevos Motuleños*—seem to be a mix of ingredients from both arid America and Arabia combined through ancient Middle Eastern culinary strategies. But that is a topic to consider later.

I've tasted, seen, and heard of traditional Middle Eastern restaurants in El Paso, Mexicali, Laredo, Ajo, and other oasis towns of the desert borderlands of the United States and Mexico. At first, I assumed that they were started up by Lebanese and Syrian refugees who landed in the American desert about a century ago, during the Ottoman conscription of Arab men into the armed forces prior to World War I. To be sure, that is exactly when Lebanese silk production collapsed, a locust plague occurred, and mass migrations of Middle Easterners began to peak in both the United States and Mexico.

My great-grandfather was one of those Syrian refugees who thought he was bound for the United States, when his steamer landed in the port of Vera Cruz, Mexico. He died not far from there before my great-grandmother, their daughter, and other kin could catch up with him, for they had properly immigrated through New York. My grandmother settled in the Midwest, while her cousins who survived Vera Cruz eventually arrived in El Paso.

Nevertheless, there is another, darker wave of Arab immigration that influenced the cultures and cuisines of Mexico and the U.S. Southwest that seldom gets aired. It began within the few decades immediately following 1492 CE and continued for a full century following the conquest of the area that is now Mexico by Hernán Cortés. Of course, 1492 marked a new era in the Americas, ushered in by Cristobal Colón's first sighting of the West Indies. Although historian Alfred Crosby has baptized it the era of the Columbian Exchange, some of my Native American friends call it the Great Colón-oscopy.

But it was also the year that tens of thousands of Jews and Moslems were forced by the Spanish Inquisition to convert to Catholicism and to leave the Iberian Peninsula or die. The Moslems who chose to convert were called Moriscos; the Jews who did so were called either Conversos or, more pejoratively, Marranos (meaning "pigs"). Within the follow-ing century, Spain lost one-third of its former population due to out-migration, disease, and mass murders that built toward genocide. Al-though many Sephardic Jews and Moorish Moslems fled to Morocco and other countries of the Maghreb, others sought refuge in the Americas.

Some of those refugees had to conceal their surnames and their re-ligious orientations from those who offered transport to the lands now known as Latin America. They took code names for their *apellidos*—animal names such as León, Garza, Gallo, Martín, Ossa, Tigre, and Zorrillo—so that others of their kind could recognize them. Others simply shifted a few consonants in their surnames to obscure their origins. (In this light, I have always wondered whether the following characters were originally of the Nabhan tribe: Juan de Navas, who fled from Granada to Zacatecas in 1621 CE; Juan Nabón y García, who left Ubeda for the sea in 1753; and Rafael Nabas, who departed Velez-Málaga for Sonora in 1782.)

Catholic on the outside, Jewish or Moslem on the inside, many of these families fled as far from the Valley of Mexico as they could when the Inquisition finally followed them to their newfound land. They took ref-uge in the most remote regions of New Spain—present-day New Mexico, Nuevo León, Chihuahua, Sonora, and Coahuila—as well as in the more remote haunts of the Yucatán Peninsula. In that first wave of immigration from Iberia to Mexico, roughly one-third of all immigrants were originally from Andalusia, where Moslems and Jews had formerly lived in the great-est numbers.

Not all of these Andalusian refugees were descendants of the Moors and Berbers who had earlier invaded southern Spain; some were true Arabs of the Umayyad dynasty. Following their defeat in 750 CE by the Abbasids, who took complete control of the House of Islam in the Middle East, these emigrants moved lock, stock, and barrel to al-Andalus to re-build their empire. The surviving Umayyad emir had both Arab and Berber in his blood, but his nostalgia was for all things Arabic. His name was Abd al-Rahman, and his longing for the taste of the Middle East was so strong that he had his sister transplant from Damascus to Córdoba his favorite fruit tree—a pomegranate—along with other seeds and livestock, so that they might grow in his surrogate empire.

Just as the Umayyad rulers transplanted the very same genetic stocks of foods from Syria, they imported chefs and their culinary treatises from the Middle East to ensure that their foodways survived intact and thrived as much as was possible. The one chef who gained the most renown in Spain for promoting Middle Eastern culinary arts was a Persian nick-named "Ziryab," referring to an entertaining blackbird of the Middle East, because of his melodious voice and dark skin. Abu al-Hasan Ali ibn Nafiʻ not only brought with him the latest cooking styles from Baghdad, but tutored the Spanish on how to present these dishes in a sequence that provided the most pleasure to one's guests. One should move from soups to tapas-size dishes of seasoned lamb and spiced fowl to desserts such as almonds, dried fruits filled with pistachios and hazelnuts, and honey-drenched pastries.

Ironically, Ziryab had been a rising star in the Abbasid court before he was warmly embraced by emir Abd al-Rahman II (the grandson) when he arrived in Córdoba in 822 CE. The emir allowed him to set the aesthetic standards for fine dining in Moorish Spain, and many later collections of recipes drew upon Ziryab's principles and predilections. His most cele-brated recipe for asparagus, *Tiqlayat ziryab*, is still prepared by Andalu-sians to this day. Seven centuries later the descendants of Abd al-Rahman and Ziryab followed much the same pattern of culinary transplantation when they were forced to relocate a second time, in the Americas. As they crossed the seas, they carried with them the Ziryab-inspired *Recetarios* as well as the great Arabic agronomy manuals such as the *Tratado* (Book of Agriculture) written by Abu Zacaria Iahia (Ibn al-ʻAwwam) around 1150 CE. One of these Persian and Arabian recipes for lamb and garbanzo stew made it all the way to Arroyo Hondo, New Mexico, where folklorist Cleofas Jaramillo recorded it in her 1939 book *The Genuine New Mexico Tasty Recipes (Potajes Sabrosas)*.

Although Jewish historians have now written more than a thousand articles on the fate of the "crypto-Jews" once they settled in the Americas, we lack an equivalent depth of scholarship about "crypto-Moslems" in the New World, who may have greatly outnumbered Jews there. At the very least, their early presence in the American deserts remains unquestioned. It can be seen in the vaulted domes, arches, and walk-in cisterns of the architecture in the desert borderlands; it can be smelled in the spices sold in the *zócolo* marketplaces that were fashioned after Middle Eastern souks; it can be drunk in the fruit-based *tesguinos* fermented much the same way *tiswin* is still brewed in the Maghreb; it can be tasted in the *alambre de carne y cafta* grilled like *laham mishwee* kababs over red-hot coals. It can be heard in the chamber music made by the plucking of the *laûd (al-ud)*, guitar (*qitarah*), and the drumming of tambores (*tanbur*)—music that accompanied the Moors and Middle Easterners into another desert realm.

Of course, Jews and Moorish and Arabic Moslems may have brought many of the same culinary practices and ingredients to the deserts of the New World. Sephardic Jewish tables in the Middle East, North Africa, and even in al-Andalus differ little from those of their Islamic neighbors, except during fasting days. The Jews and Moslems who escaped the Inquisition by taking refuge in the far recesses of the American deserts could import a few foodstuffs and spices from their brethren remaining in the Mediterranean region, but for the most part they had to grow their own.

And grow they did. By the 1750s, at least twenty-seven food crop species first cultivated in the Old World had made it to the Sonoran Desert. According to plant geographer William Dunmire, they included some crops of the Middle East, Maghreb, and al-Andalus that did not otherwise come with the English or French into other parts of North America: millet, black-eyed pea, citron, lime, and sour orange. For the most part, crypto-Jews and crypto-Moslems carried with them the same species, but different varieties of seeds and breeds. Moreover, their uses were distinctive.

One distinctive trait of Sephardic and Arabic culinary legacies is the use of deeply memorable, somewhat pungent spice mixtures with meats, fishes, fowl, soups, and breads. The spice mixtures used in the Old World include these classic composites: *baharat*, of cinnamon, allspice, and cloves; *chat masala*, of cardamom, black pepper, cumin, and cinnamon; *hnot*, of cumin, tumeric, mace, nutmeg, cayenne, cloves, rose petals, orange peel, and green anise seed; *ras al hanout*, of cinnamon, cardamom, mace, nutmeg, paprika pepper, black pepper, turmeric, and ground ginger; and *zaatar*, of wild thyme, oregano or marjoram, sumac, sesame seeds, and salt.

It is but a short hop, skip, and jump from these Old World mixtures to the Mexican mixtures prepared for various *moles*. For example, a classic red mole spice mixture for turkey includes cinnamon, black pepper, anise seed, sesame seeds, cloves, salt, and various chilis. A green *mole pipian* mixture might include cloves, bay leaves, thyme, marjoram, salt, pumpkin seeds, cumin seeds, and chili peppers. These mixtures vary in a few details from place to place in Mexico, just as they do in the Maghreb and the Middle East, but they are discernible *as mixtures* and *in the mouth*. In short, moles cannot be viewed as a purely Mesoamerican invention, for they were probably the first sophisticated examples of Mediterranean/ Mesoamerican fusion cuisine.

In a small breakfast café in New Mexico last year, I learned how such fusions occur spontaneously again and again, while their origins become obscured by hype that seeks to offer simple sound bites about fashionable foods. At Pasqual's for breakfast one morning, my wife, Laurie, and I were seated at the same table where a party of New Yorkers had begun to order their fare; multiple parties at a single long table is common procedure at Pasqual's. One of the folks at our table was obviously a food writer and took the lead on recommendations.

"You *simply must* order the huevos Motuleños—it is an ancient Mayan dish that I first had in Merida on a food tour of the Yucatán Peninsula."

That comment piqued my curiosity, so I perused the menu to find this Mayan dish. It certainly sounded interesting and indeed is very flavorful, but after scanning the ingredients I was sure that Mayan it was not. The recipe for this breakfast dish actually has more Old World ingredients in it—onions, ham, plantains, peas, eggs, and cheese—than New World ingredients—black beans, corn tortillas, tomatoes, and habanero chili peppers. Something was fishy in Santa Fe.

Later that same year I traveled with my daughter to Merida to meet some of the friends she had made the previous summer while researching Arab immigration to the Yucatán Peninsula. The first morning there she took me for a long walk before breakfast, past the old stone walls sweating and stained with black fungus; past rubber trees and tropical fruits; past shops selling colorful *huipiles* for women and guayabera shirts for men; past butcher shops where achiote paste was being plastered onto sides of ham for making *cochinita pibil*.

"This is no desert," I mumbled to myself as the humidity started to rise and my shirt plastered itself to my back. "This is about as far away from Tucson and Santa Fe as the moon is from the earth."

We made it past a marketplace, and Laura began looking for a small breakfast café she wanted me to know. At last we entered the door of Café Siqueff; it was actually the second Café Siqueff, for the first had been in the small town of Motul, not too far outside of Merida. That was where don Jorge Siqueff, a Lebanese chef, and his wife, a Mayan woman from Motul, first brought an altogether odd assortment of ingredients together to improvise a breakfast for don Felipe Carrillo Puerto in 1959.

Don Felipe savored that concoction of Old World and New World ingredients as it crossed his lips and lingered on his palette. He suggested to his friend don Jorge that the café might want to offer this breakfast dish on a regular basis.

Today, don Jorge's creation, huevos Motuleños, is served in nearly every restaurant in Merida as well as in many restaurants in Santa Fe, Albuquerque, and Tucson. But at Café Siqueff, it remains on the menu alongside the same dishes that were in don Jorge's repertoire when he and his wife improvised the breakfast that made Motul famous in 1959: *huevos Arabes*, *kibi crudo*, *eftoyer*, and *labne*. And some of these dishes predate recent Lebanese and Syrian immigration to Yucatán, perhaps back to the founding of Merida in 1542.

By 1580, one-third of Merida's Spanish-speaking population was from al-Andalus. And yet most of them spoke in other tongues when they were in the safety of their own homes. They spoke Mozarabic, the lingua franca back home in al-Andalus, and read a written language called *aljamiado*. Some of them may have known Ladino as well, for their neighbors had been Jewish Conversos at the time of the Inquisition. And when their mouths were not speaking in these tongues, they were filled with flavors from their forefather's homelands.

Wild thyme and oregano, sesame and anise seed.

Today, on the Yucatán Peninsula, when a Mayan shaman offers a bit of distilled honey spirits to the gods in the form of a liqueur known as Xtabentun, its sole flavoring is ground anise seed. It has the fragrance of *araq*, the anisette that my grandfather and uncles bootlegged even after they had arrived in the Americas. The anise they used is said to have come from my family's ancestral grounds in the Holy Lands.

It has found its way to holiness in another land as well.

CHAPTER 3

Chasing Alice Ann

Arabic Terms Leaping Languages and Oceans

THERE ARE ECHOES—aural mirages—most anywhere you go in the American *deserta*. Early in my time as a pilgrim and apprentice of the Sonoran Desert, I began to hear such echoes, not knowing from whence they were emanating. I would also see mirages of places that seemed to belong to another world, but it was years before I realized their origins. Echoes and mirages give the desert its special soundscape, its peculiar hues.

The source of some of these echoes was first revealed to me when I was working to record the many Spanish, English, and O'odham names for places scattered around the Gran Desierto along the Arizona-Sonora border. It was during a time when I had the pleasure of interviewing O'odham elders who had traveled the land between Yuma, Gila Bend, Quitovac, Caborca, and Baboquivari before a fence ran along the borderline. I had begun to compare the place-names that these elders recalled with ones that the first Jesuit padres in the region had recorded in their clumsy transcriptions some three centuries earlier. And I had been attempting to pin these names to places on the map, some of which were vitally important to desert dwellers: springs, seeps, wells, and kiss tanks, or *tinajas*. I had learned where some of these features were from Julian Hayden, Bill Broyles, Ofelia Zepeda, Fillman Bell, and Richard Felger, who had located them during their many trips along the Camino del Diablo and other ancient trails across the desert.

As I drove alone across the desert one summer—on my way to pick up my children in Yuma for a weekend in the Baboquivaris—I was particularly absorbed by an effort to understand the linguistic patterns that underlie O'odham place-names. In essence, I was trying to sense the morphology of words and phrases that describe the morphology of the desert itself. I was particularly curious about how rather obscure water features found amidst vast tracts of waterless land are named in the Hia c-eḍ O'odham dialect.

For starters, I knew that the suffix -ik or -ag or -ig was often added to nouns describing a key physical or ecological feature of a landscape, in such a way that -ic might be loosely translated as "place of." And so, as I headed west around the northern edges of the Baboquivaris, I came close to S-keg'iibhaig, "Place of Many Prickly Pear Fruits," and Ba:banag, "Place of Many Coyotes." To the south and west of the Baboquivaris, there were villages now called Cu:lik and Cowulic (formerly Kavul-ik), both of these names holding the pattern. Cowul-ik is also the old name for Caborca, Sonora.

Then, as I passed Sells and headed toward Covered Wells, I came upon another name, Nolik, that gave me pause. I had seen it listed on old Spanish-language maps as Las Norias, "Well Hoists" or "Waterwheels." Apparently, the suffix -ik had been added to the contraction of a loan word, noria, that had come into the region with immigrants from the Iberian Peninsula, immigrants who had brought with them a water-lifting technology from the Old World.

So, I surmised, the morphology of place-names in the O'odham language could neatly accommodate concepts, images, and technologies that originated in distant lands, especially where those features had somehow gained relevance to the way the Desert People themselves could live on their own land.

I traveled westward to Ajo, northward to Gila Bend, and southwestward to Yuma, reciting the names of places on either side of the highway as I passed them. To refresh my memory, I would occasionally glance at a map and draft gazetteer that Broyles, Felger, and I had been working on that described and located the place-names of the Gran Desierto. Most of the terms were ones that I could translate from O'odham ha-neokĭ into English and Spanish, and most were landscape features that I myself had visited. However, one particular name puzzled me because I did not know what it meant in O'odham. Furthermore, I had never been to the particular place that desert writer and itinerant geographer Bill Broyles thought was associated with this name, Aguaje de los Alquives, a waterhole south of the Gila River that may be between Dripping Springs or Baker Tanks.

Neither could I immediately find the term alquives in a Spanish dictionary. As I passed into the landscape in which this locality was said to be hidden, something struck me as exceedingly odd—yet at the same time anciently familiar—about this term.

When I queried Broyles by phone, he was rather matter-of-fact about it: "I'm pretty sure it's the watering place used by the Anglo ranchers of the early twentieth century between the Gila River and Baker Tanks. Many early explorers, padres, and soldiers watered their animals there. And it seems the name used by some old Sand Papago nomads, *algibes*, comes from an old Spanish term *aljibe*, translated in one reference I have as 'cistern.' I don't know much more about it. . . . Hey, man, it's all yours."

That night I looked up *aljibe* instead of *alquives* in a Spanish dictionary. An abbreviated annotation in the dictionary entry caught my eye: "from Arabic, meaning walk-in cistern." This little piece of trivia lodged itself in my memory. It did not resurface again until I found myself in the Arab-speaking village where my grandfather had been born. There in the Anti-Lebanon mountain range spanning the border between Lebanon and Syria, I found the missing piece of the puzzle.

I was trying to walk out from our ancestral village with one of my cousins, but we were not getting very far very fast. After two straight nights of feasting, I needed some exercise, and I thought I would go alone to roam one of the two limestone ridges that sandwiched the village into a narrow canyon. However, this one cousin of mine had caught me sneaking out the back door, and he decided that I needed an escort and guide. My guess is that he feared I would get lost on my own, stumble into some other clan's territory, and embarrass the entire Nabhan clan with my lack of geographic orientation.

And so we began to walk, but would get only twenty or thirty yards before he pointed to a slope, a promontory, or a watercourse and stopped to tell me a story about it.

"Look, right there, that is the land your father deeded back to us after he realized that your grandfather had inherited it, for he had the foresight to know that none of you would ever come back to farm it again."

"Gary Baul, come over here, there is water hidden here that I want to show you."

My family was apparently full of water-witchers. They were keenly interested in the places where underground aquifers came close to the surface, Such places made my cousin's wishbone-shaped willow wand twitch and then plunge downward. We slipped between two limestone outcrops and came out into a small opening on the ridge. It was shielded from view in every direction by the outcrops so that no one above us or even below us in the village could see us, let alone the water hidden beneath us. Here in this natural amphitheater was a hole in the ground that looked as though it had literally been cut down through the limestone.

"It is natural," my cousin said. "A natural well. You can walk down into it if you like."

"Walk into a well?" I asked. "Won't I fall into it?"

"No, you walk down into the shade, let your eyes adjust, and then you see the water in the well below. It is protected from the burning sun. That's why it never dries up."

We walked down a dozen foot-worn limestone steps, descending below a rocky ledge that overhung the well itself. Was it really a well? Or was it a spring or a storage pit where rainwater collected below ground level after those rare but essential torrential rains?

"What do you call this kind of place where you get water? What is its name in Arabic?" I asked.

"Gary Baul, this is family well, but we give it no special name. We don't name it Nabhan Well. We do nothing like that. We have many places hidden like this, where we must go for water during time of war or trouble."

"But what do you call this kind of well or water hole?"

"As I already say to you, cousin, nothing special: *al-Jubb*."

My brain synapses fired in a pattern unlike the ones they had ever made before as my thoughts suddenly leaped from Lebanon to southern Arizona and back again: *al-Jubb* > *aljibe* > *alquives*. Arabic > Andalusian Spanish and Sonoran Spanish > O'odham. As I put these patterns in place, a river of questions flooded my mind: Had an Arabic term come to Moorish Spain with the Umayyads in the ninth century after their Islamic empire fell in Damascus? Did they introduce this term for shaded cisterns to Spanish-language speakers in Andalusia, who transmogrified it and made it their own? And when all unconverted Moslems and Jews were expelled by Ferdinand and Isabella from the Iberian Peninsula in 1492, did they take the term with them to the Americas as they escaped the subsequent Spanish Inquisition? And when exactly did the term land in the Sonoran Desert of western North America and become absorbed into the O'odham tongue of the Uto-Aztecan language family, one unique to the New World? Why had it seemed familiar to me? Had I ever heard my grandfather or my uncles speak the term *al-Jubb* when I was growing up?

My Lebanese cousin had unknowingly gifted me with a lens through which I could see my own American landscape freshly. I could use this lens to look at words commonly spoken around me in the desert, words in O'odham, in vernacular Spanish, and even in American cowboy lingo. I soon learned that *al-Jubb* > *aljibe* > *alquives* is not the only chain that connects Arabic with O'odham. The chain *al-nāʿurah* > *annora* > *noria* > *no:lik*, "waterwheel," is another, running from classic Arabic to Andalusian Spanish to Mexican Spanish to O'odham. From my fellow Lebanese American writer Habeeb Salloum, I also learned that the term commonly used for "irrigation ditch" in both Spanish and several indigenous languages, *acequia*, is a loaner from the Arabic *al-saqiyah*. Likewise, the word for "artificial pool" used in Sonora, *alberca*, came from the Arabic *al-birkah*; Sonorans hardly ever use the Latin-derived term *piscine*. At least ten Arabic-derived terms for managing and conserving water are still found in common usage in the Sonoran Desert—whether in Spanish or English or Native American languages. They have found utility in a thirsty land some five thousand miles away from their original home ground.

The chains connecting Arabic with O'odham are not restricted to water words. They also include terms for fruits and other foods, like those for apricots, *al-barquq* > *albaricoque* > *wi:ragogi*; for dates, *tiin* > *tuna* > *suuna*; for peaches, *duraq* > *durazno* > *julash*; and for oranges, *naranj* > *naranja* > *narash*.

I learned some of these names for fruit from don Luciano Noriega, the last full-time O'odham farmer at the oasis of Quitovac, Sonora. He tended an orchard at Quitovac that would make any Arab feel at home, for it offered dates, pomegranates, figs, and shade to all who were lured to its verdure. It harbored wild and weedy plants as well. Luciano once showed me the sulfur-hued blossoms of some safflower plants that had cropped up after a truck going by the oasis had spilled some seeds out onto the roadside.

Like a dry wind, he whispered that the "native" name for this introduced safflower was *sasafrani*. It was a Papago-ized version of the Spanish *azafrán*, rooted in the Arabic *az-zaʿfarān*, which originally referred to saffron blossoms and their golden pistils, not to safflower. The word *az-*

za'farān is derived from an ancestral tongue that Arabic and other Semitic languages had as their precursor, which linguists refer to as proto-Semitic. Luciano also taught me the Spanish name for another plant introduced from the Mediterranean, one known in English as heron's bill or in botanical Latin as *Erodium cicutarium*. In the Sonoran Desert, where it occasionally carpets the sandy stretches of arroyos after winter rains, it is called *alfilería* in Sonoran Spanish and *filaree* in southwestern English. The same plant is called *al-hilel* wherever it carpets Arabian sands today.

Don Luciano did not merely observe plants and name them; he also used some of them for his own hedonistic pleasure. He fermented cactus into wine and corn into beer. Although he typically used an ancient O'odham term for these drinks, *nawait*, he collectively referred to them as *tesguino* in conversations with his Sonoran neighbors or with visitors from other indigenous tribes. I doubt he knew that this term harkens all the way back to mildly fermented palm wines of the Middle East, still called *tiswin* among many Arab-speaking tribes. Neither did he know that his *casa de adobe* had bricks in it that my Lebanese grandfather would have called *at-tubb* or that the barrio he lived in would have been called a *barri* if it had been an Arabic neighborhood.

What a wonderful feeling it was for me to hear an indigenous elder in my adopted homeland echo words that my ancestors would have used as they wandered from Yemen to Oman to Jordan and then to Syria and Lebanon over the centuries! Don Luciano—who first taught me about the desert's herbs and gums—had filled a role in my life that my grandfather, if he had lived longer, might otherwise have played. I retained some memory of my grandfather's voice as he peddled fruit and drank bootlegged *araq* anisette in "the new country," even though he died when I was just five. Whenever I heard don Luciano's whispered litany of plant names as we walked through the desert together, I thought of what I had lost by not having more time in the wild with my own grandparents.

And yet O'odham is not the only Native American language that has loan words from Arabic so identifiable that it sometimes seems that they did not even pass through Spanish. While traveling among the Rarámuri, or Tarahumara, in the Chihuahuan Sierras of northern Mexico, I learned that they call their spike fiddle a *raveli*, a term clearly derived from the Arabic *rebab* or *rababah*. No wonder I hear echoes!

Oddly, I had to learn of the Arabic words embedded in the O'odham and Rarámuri lexicon before I fully appreciated that they were also lodged in the vernacular English of the desert Southwest, particularly in what is known as "cowboy lingo." Robert Smead's recently published *Vocabulario Vaquero / Cowboy Lingo* suggests that there are as many terms derived from Arabic terms in the southwestern cowboy lexicon as in Native American languages and more than in any other language aside from Hispanicized Latin. I began listening to such lingo after I moved to one of the great old ranching communities of the U.S.–Mexico borderlands in 1975, when I worked on the Research Ranch on the Sonoita Plains near Elgin, Arizona. My wife and I now keep horses, sheep, and turkeys and have even more frequent contact with working cowboys, ranchers, and large-animal veterinarians who use terms for livestock that were first introduced into the region more than three centuries ago.

Some of the ranchers who have cowboyed for years with Sonoran vaqueros use these ancient terms as casually and nonchalantly as my children use computerspeak. They still refer to a horseman of exceptional skill as "one damn fine *jinete.*" In doing so, they are maintaining a tradition of honoring a fluid style of riding developed in North Africa by Berbers; the term now refers not to the style, but to the rider himself. It comes through Sonoran Spanish as *xinete,* which is in turn lent from the Andalusian *zanāti,* an echo of the name of the Berber-speaking Zanatah tribe of Algeria, encoded in the Arabic *Zeneti.*

Sonoran and Arizonan vaqueros may still call their packsaddle an *albardón,* derived from the Iberian term *albarda,* which in turn came from the Arabic *al-barda'a.* Among the other tack such cowboys use is a leather belt they call an *ación*—from the Arabic *as-siyur.* A whip they call an *azote* comes from the Arabic *as-sût.* Ringing straps are called *argollas,* from *al-gulla.* My favorite Arabic-derived term for tack has always been the one used widely for a headstall or rope halter, *hackamore.* It comes straight from the Andalusian *jaquima,* which echoes the ancient Arabic *sakima,* for "something worn on the head."

Many color terms in Spanish, English, and Native American languages are traceable to Arab origins. But because color-blindness is among the many flaws I have as a human being, it took me a while before I began to hear the terms cowboys use for the hide colors of horses, cattle, and even sheep. I simply could not discern all of the subtleties of hue that fascinated the horsemen I rode with in Sonora, Chihuahua, and Arizona. I could certainly pick out an *almagre*, a rust-colored stallion, and knew that the term came from *al-magra*, "red earth." I could see a sulfur-colored *azafrán*, from *az-za'farān*. But there were other colors in the palette I simply could not see.

"Could you chase me down that Alice Ann?" a cowboy once asked me when we were saddling up a whole remuda of horses he'd just brought in to take for a trail ride into the sierras.

I stood still. I blinked. My mouth was dry. I said nothing, but kept looking for a mare named Alice Ann for whom this cowboy had particular affection. But all I could see at first was a mess of geldings and studs.

"Could you just go and get that Alice Ann over there by the gate?" He repeated and sighed.

I scanned the corral, and closest to the gate was one young reddish-brown mare with a tail and mane of about the same tone as her hide, a horse I had missed seeing the first time around.

"Is that the girl you want?" I pointed.

"Yeah, that sorrel filly. You talk some Mexican, don't you? You know, *alazán*. Bring her here."

I sidled up to her and while quietly whispering "Alice Ann" into her ears slung the hackamore around her neck. She didn't flinch, so I placed the *bosal* over her nose, popped her ears in between two straps that I adjusted until they fit. I grabbed the horse-hair *mecate* reins and coaxed her into walking along with me. While I led her over to where the saddles were hung on the stacked mesquite fence of the corral, I pondered the term that buckaroo had used, *alazán*. I tried to keep it in my own head until I got back home that night. I looked it up in my big dictionary from the Spanish Academy.

Sure enough, "Alice Ann" was of Middle Eastern descent, with *al-azár*—the reddish color of wood—hidden in its etymology.

There she was, right in front of me, an Arabian I should have recognized by sound and sight. But as a poet-blogger who is nicknamed "Jac" recently reminded me with his limerick, Alice Ann need not be a she:

On the frontier a cowboy's best pal
Was called Alice Ann, and not Sal.

The trick is, of course,
That this friend was a horse
So an Alice could be a male pal.

The drumming of hooves as Alice Ann galloped down the wadi echoed off the banks of the down-cut arroyo.

CHAPTER 4

Oasis Time

From the Sonoran to the Sahara,
Following Doctor Forbes

In the open desert plain,
With its wild parsimonious beauty . . .
Every bush and stone,
Every beetle and lizard,
Every track of jerboa, gazelle,
Or ostrich on the sand,
Becomes of value and is remembered,
It may be years afterwards,
While the stones of the campfire
Stand black and deserted,
In testimony of the brief season
Of love.
—Wilfred Scawen Blunt, *The Seven Golden Odes of Pagan Arabia*
(1903)

THE LIZARD AND BEETLE tracks covered the face of the dune like crazed
Arabic calligraphy, but their scribes were nowhere to be seen. It was too
cold for long-tailed lizards and scarab beetles to poke their heads above
the surface of the sand. I was shivering, waiting for an early January sun to
rise, wondering how the air could be so chilly and wet if this indeed were
the Desert of all deserts, the Sah'ra. It was both foggy and windy, and my
Berber guides were discomforted enough that they had not stepped outside their old beat-up Toyota Land Cruiser since the moment we had
arrived at the crest of the dune a half-hour ago. Instead, they huddled
together inside the vehicle, out of the wind's reach, their hands plunged
down into the pockets of their robes, chanting along with a cassette tape of
the Qu'ran, offering their own call to prayer to the vast sea of sand that lay

before us. As I perched myself atop an enormous dune that overlooks the ancient oasis of Siwa, Egypt, I tried to recall how I got here and, in particular, how I had first learned of this Doctor Forbes, whose ghost I had chased to this place halfway around the world from my own desert home.

As I recalled, it had something to do with the godmother of my daughter, Laura, a woman who was already in her nineties when she sprinkled holy water on the baby at a baptism out in a desert arroyo at dawn in the summer of 1984. Her name was Laura Kerman, and she probably would have died later that baptism day had I not successfully performed the Heimlich maneuver on her after a bunch of beans got caught in her gullet and she began to suffocate. A potter, folk artist, singer, storyteller, and Catholic catechist, she proved quite resilient following that near-death experience, staying up and singing rain-bringing songs to us late into the night. Rain came, of course. Tohono O'odham by blood, she was a bridge between cultures by inclination. As a young woman, she had worked in Tucson, Arizona, as a maid, cook, and companion for Doctor Forbes and his ailing wife in the years just prior to the Forbeses' move to Egypt in 1918.

I suppose that because Laura Kerman had spent time as a member of the Forbes household and then, some seven decades later, of my own, she had always wanted me and Doctor Forbes to meet. Why I later pursued Doctor Forbes's legacy had as much to do with Laura as it did with Forbes himself. But just as there was nothing straightforward in following Doctor Forbes down his rambling path, it was never easy knowing how to satisfy Miss Laura Kerman. The first time I arrived at her desert home, I turned and began to walk away after noticing the sign by her gate that announced, "BY APPOINTMENT ONLY." And then I heard a voice arise from what I learned later was her pottery-making shed.

"Excuse me, young man, do you wish to see me?"

"Yes . . . well, may I get your phone number so that I can make an appointment to come and talk with you?"

"I don't have a telephone! Why don't you talk to me now?"

"Well, because I don't think I have a previously arranged appointment with you . . . "

"Oh, just come on in! I put that sign up there so I can keep away bill collectors and the bureaucrats from the BIA."

Perhaps it was during that first visit that Laura told me how I reminded her of Doctor Forbes, given my preoccupation with enduring seeds and hardy crops and all things desert adapted. However, when Laura lauded the deceased desert scientist for his elegance—something I clearly lacked —I wondered if I were like him at all. Even on Tucson's hottest summer days, Doctor Forbes wore black suits, black ties, and black shoes around town as if he were a desert raven. He would don a Stetson or Panama hat most days as well. He would always dress "up," she said, unless his work that day was to be with the stinkin' hot desert itself, and then he would dress "down" a bit, in dungarees with suspenders, boots, and collarless muslin work shirts.

Laura fondly remembered how he had brought back from Egypt certain plants—millet, lentils, salt cedars—that her family had tried to grow around their dooryard garden in a desert valley just below Baboquivari Peak. None except the salt cedar had persisted by the time I met Laura decades later. She proudly announced to me that even though some of his plant introductions were duds, Doctor Forbes had been the first man known to climb that sacred peak in 1898, after his Tucson-born fiancé, Georgie Scott, humorously claimed that she would not marry him unless he made a successful ascent of Baboquivari. Laura also cackled as she told me that when Dr. Forbes lit a fire atop the sacred mountain to announce his successful ascent, a drunken neighbor of hers saw the fire and pronounced that the world was coming to an end. At age eighty-one, Doctor Forbes climbed Baboquivari again fifty years after his first successful ascent and less than two years after Georgie passed away.

In short, Doctor Forbes had become something of a legend in my home state of Arizona. To my knowledge, however, no other Arizonan was fool enough to follow him literally from one desert oasis to the next, from the New World to the Old, and back again.

I had begun my tenure in the desert much as Forbes himself had done, traveling frequently to remote agricultural oases in search of desert-adapted seeds. Forbes had come in 1896, fresh out of the University of Chicago with a Ph.D. in botany, ready to develop the first agricultural college in the Sonoran Desert. He arrived in Tucson by train at two in the morning and found no one there to meet him at the station. With all his baggage in tow, he hiked a mile in a dust storm to the new University of Arizona campus. Unable to find the university's entrance gate, he slipped between strands of barbed wire and made his way to the only office building on campus. There he waited in his dust-covered, rumpled suit until morning, when he met the college president, signed in on the payroll, and began work that very day.

Over the next three decades, Doctor Forbes visited many ancient desert farming villages in Arizona, Sonora, and Baja California for clues as to what crops would do best in the Sonoran Desert. He became convinced that all desert farmers could learn much from one another, but at the same time he recognized that Sonoran Desert oases were peculiar in their similarities to those in northern Africa. At San Ignacio, Baja California, he noted, "we came to the crest of a low ridge [and] at the same moment the palm-filled oasis appeared in its widest place;—great bunches of red and yellow fruit being apparent even at a distance of a mile. The whole effect of this first view was strikingly Moorish. The innumerable feathery topped palms, the low, flat roofed houses, the church with its dome over the altar, the irregular roads . . . are much like the current views of North Africa."

I, too, came to the University of Arizona campus from the Chicago area, but merely as someone who had somehow been allowed into college without a high school diploma or GED. Within a few weeks of living in Tucson, I was plowing through the early archives of Doctor Forbes's team of agricultural explorers, trying to learn just what crops one could grow in the Stinkin' Hot Desert without having to do Heimlich maneuvers on them every day. With a list compiled from those early University of Arizona Agricultural Experiment Station bulletins that had been edited by Doctor Forbes, I began to wander out to the Hispanic and Native American oases of the desert on both sides of the Arizona-Sonora border, trading for the very same seeds that Forbes and his farm staff had first described to science.

One particular oasis that intrigued me was just south of the Sonoran border some thirty-five miles and had been continuously inhabited by the O'odham for centuries and centuries. The Mexicans called it Quitovac; the O'odham themselves simply referred to its spring-fed marshy lagoon as Va:k, "Out in Tules," for you had to cross some thirty miles of absolutely dry desert from any direction to get to it. It was there that I fully realized that O'odham and Hispanic farmers harbored not only desert-adapted seeds of the New World, but some from the Old World as well. Below an irrigation ditch that led from the artesian springs of Quitovac, an elderly O'odham farmer named Luciano Noriega would take me around to visit his irrigated waffle gardens time after time that I visited him. As if I had never really seen them before, he would show me each of the pomegranates, figs, apricots, and dates that lined the elevated edges of each waffle or "hod" in his garden. In the shade of these hardy trees, Luciano had sown annual crops such as lentils, peas, garbanzos, and cilantro during the winter time.

I've never been sure that Luciano consciously knew that his winter plantings were Old World crops because over the previous three centuries his ancestors had "O'odham-ized" the Arabic-derived Spanish names for these crops introduced by missionaries from the Mediterranean basin. In the summer, however, Luciano grew mostly the New World crops, including sixty-day maize, tepary beans, cushaw squashes, and big cheese pumpkins.

After Luciano finally passed away and none of his nephews kept up his garden at Quitovac, I grew thirsty to see a well-tended oasis garden once again, wherever it might be in the world. I had my first opportunity to quench that thirst on a trip with my wife and kids to Egypt and Lebanon in 2000. We were dazzled by the beauty of many date palm groves and dooryard gardens while riding a felucca down the Nile, but of course they did not have all the features that true islandlike oases demonstrated. Nevertheless, after getting off the felucca and visiting the ancient harbor of Alexandria, we heard that it was the jumping-off point for caravans to a true oasis located far out in the western desert, near the Libyan border. Its contemporary name was Siwa, but it had also been called the "Giant Grove of Palm Trees" and the "Land of the Olives" (Tehenu) in various languages at different points in history. If I ever had the chance to return to Egypt, I told myself then, I would make a date to visit that place.

My vow was fulfilled just four years later. Father Dave Denny, a Carmelite priest who is fluent in Arabic, agreed to accompany me out to Siwa. But before I departed for Egypt, I remembered that the Arizona Historical Society archives had both photos and articles written by Doctor Forbes regarding his time in Egypt. I had frequently used his article on O'odham lima beans grown in Egypt that I had found in these archives, but vaguely remembered that he had also written something on oasis agriculture in Egypt. However, until I started to rummage through the many Forbes papers with friends, I hadn't realized that his most extensive commentaries were on Siwa itself!

Doctor Forbes had spent an entire month there in 1919 and upon his return to the United States had gone on a lecture circuit throughout the Southwest to talk about the lessons he had learned there. I could see from his lecture notes and published articles that he felt as though the Siwan Berbers and Bedouins provided the ultimate models for an ethic of water conservation in the desert. After being shocked at the rather extravagant use of water that was rapidly becoming the norm among Arizona farmers and urbanites, he was humbled to see how careful the Siwans were in using their artesian spring water, even though they had some two hundred springs scattered across their oasis basin. Forbes championed the Siwan example, for he apparently had become grief stricken by the groundwater pumping that had dramatically accelerated in the Southwest during his several years' absence from Arizona. He prophetically argued that unless Arizonans curbed their use of fossil fuel to extract water from the earth below them, they would eventually ruin the very land they were attempting to make productive and turn the Sonoran Desert into something that looked more like the shifting sands of the Sah'ra than Siwa's own verdure.

Just before Father Dave and I departed for Egypt, I arranged to get copied as many of Doctor Forbes's photos of Siwa as possible to take as gifts to the Siwan community. From the photos and their captions, it appeared that a Siwan sheikh named Hammam had hosted Doctor Forbes; together they had made a map detailing the location of every date palm, olive tree, and vegetable bed at Sheikh Hammam's gardenlike grove at a place Forbes called Ain Zeidan. Perhaps by showing contemporary Siwans photos of the sheikh, I could find one of his descendants who might recall Siwan oral history about Doctor Forbes's time there.

Traveling to the Siwa oasis from Alexandria or Cairo is an eight- to eleven-hour excursion today, but took five to seven days during Doctor Forbes's era. Father Dave and I took one bus to Marsa Matruh and another from the coastal city inland across barren *gibbel* plains to Siwa. Forbes, however, had to find a ship that would sail for three days from Alexandria to Marsa Matruh; then he had to head southward across the desert, carrying his supplies first by Model T and later by camel. After he had arrived at Siwa for a month-long stay, he conceded that he and his camel hadn't exactly bonded with one another:

Of the camel I am not competent to speak, except to say that he is the most unlovely combination of contradictory qualities. He makes up for his personal shortcomings, however, by his endurance of desert conditions . . . [eating] the thorny argool and other desert vegetation, and finding much of his water supply in the dew and fog condensed upon it.

[And yet,] it is not among the privileges of white men to understand the camel, and consequently, much grief results from their contact with each other. The camel bites very viciously and his bite is very poisonous, for he does not brush his teeth and his mouth is very dirty. . . .

The brute grunts and protests and pretends to be about to bite, then sinks slowly to his knees then to his haunches, where he can be mounted by stepping on his neck and jumping backward up into the saddle. When you are safely in your seat you encourage the beast by making a noise something like a boa constrictor trying to hiss with a pig in his gullet. Then you pitch forward as his haunches rise, and backward as his shoulders come up, and guiding your camel by the halter or a stick, you go undulating off across the desert with a sea sickly motion that all hinges in the small of your back.

You can perhaps imagine about how I felt at the end of my first day's ride in company with a bunch of natives before whom it was necessary to preserve an appearance of sang froid at all times.

Although Doctor Forbes could not keep up with the nomadic Awlad Ali tribe of Arab-speaking Bedu and their camels, he was impressed by their management of dromedaries, sheep, and goats. Not surprisingly, he compared their skills to the only desert dwellers he had previously known who had analogous traditional ecological knowledge: "I used to say that the Papago [O'odham] Indians were the best stockmen in the Southwest; but now I believe the Arabs are the finest on the face of the earth."

Once Doctor Forbes arrived in Siwa, he felt far more at home with the agriculturally oriented Berbers there than he did with the Bedouin; in fact, the Berbers hardly used camels, preferring to travel in two-wheeled carts pulled by one or two donkeys. On our first day in Siwa, a young Berber offered to arrange for us a "taxi" to find the gardens of Ain Zeidan that Forbes had mapped. When the "taxi" arrived, it was a cart pulled by a donkey named Muhammad, who seemed to have picked up some of the "camel attitude" that Doctor Forbes had described so well. When our taxi driver saw the eighty-four-year-old photos of Doctor Forbes and the sheikh together beneath the palms of Ain Zeidan, he decided to take us to see the grandson of the sheikh in the photos, a young man named Ahmed Jerry Hammam, who agreed to accompany us to his grandfather's date grove.

Now, with four of us in the cart, the donkey was none too happy, but he eventually galloped his way back to the housing compound nearest to the palm groves of Ain Zeidan. Ahmed Jerry saw three old men sitting in the shade of an ancient mud wall, ordered the donkey to halt, and ran over to talk to them. Soon he led back to the cart a gray-haired elder dressed in white from head to foot—slippers, robe, fez, and all.

"This," Ahmed Jerry announced in broken English, "he the last living son of the sheikh you see in the bicture. Show him bicture."

It happened that I was showing the old man the first photo he had ever seen of his father, who had died some four decades earlier. The old man looked and looked at the photo, and then began to cry. We all looked off to the date groves on the horizon. When the old man recovered, he quietly asked Ahmed Jerry a question.

"He say, when bicture taken?"

"Doctor Forbes came here in 1919. 1919, the picture was taken."

Ahmed Jerry translated our response into Berber for the old man. The old man offered a brief commentary in Berber and then gestured to see if he could keep the photo. We nodded. Ahmed Jerry explained, "My uncle, he say bicture made the year before he born. He never know the other man, because he not born yet. Never hear his *baba* tell story of Ameerikani."

After some small talk, Ahmed Jerry told his uncle that we would be going on to the date grove. The old man hugged us, kissed us, blessed us, and let us pass. Minutes later the donkey cart stopped in front of a small mechanical pump that had once been used to transfer artesian spring water from a holding basin into the irrigation ditches that led out into the grove. The basin was contaminated with motor oil, the pump was broken, and some unirrigated palms were dying.

Disappointment must have flooded across my face. Compared to other, immaculately tended date palm groves we had seen in Siwa, Ain Zeidan had fallen into disrepair. Few of the date palms and olive trees had been pruned in recent years, and only a few of the hods had annual crops growing in them. Ahmed Jerry led us through them nonetheless, taking us over to one particular palm and stopping below it.

"This one. It look like date balm in bicture of my grandfather."

I glanced at Father Dave, and he glanced back at me. It was unlikely that it was the very same date palm that was in the eighty-five-year-old photo, but . . .

"Would like Father Dave to take a picture? You and me? Together under the palm tree?" I asked.

"*Shukran*," he answered, thanking us in Arabic. I squatted next to him in the shade of the date palm, wishing I had a pith helmet like the one Doctor Forbes had worn during his era in Egypt. Father Dave clicked the shutter and then came over to Ahmed Jerry to show him the digital image on the back of the camera. Ahmed Jerry looked satisfied. An obscured relationship between Arizonans and Siwans had somehow been renewed.

I only wished that the date grove itself and the gardens found in its shade had been renewed since the time Doctor Forbes had seen it because his description of its productivity in its prime had been mouth watering: "In the basins of Ain Zeidan gardens . . . there were growing in September, olive trees, lemons, oranges, grapes, tomatoes, eggplant, tobacco, peppers, *bamia* (okra), squash, water-melon, sweet-melon, cucumber, apricot, millets, alfalfa (*bersim hegazi*), parsnip, purslane, Jews mallow (*muhlukiya*) and tree cotton [hibiscus]. In winter, wheat, barley, onions, garlic, and broad beans are grown. On the salty borders stand figs, pomegranates and date palms."

Regarding the resourcefulness of the Siwan Berbers who tended these gardens, Doctor Forbes had added that "these desert peoples maintain themselves in comfort and a considerable degree of civilization on a water supply that is all derived from a six inch rainfall. This is suggestive of the great latent values yet to be developed in our own arid regions in time to come."

Within hours of my disappointment over the condition of Ain Zeidan, however, I stumbled upon another date grove and garden that still had the diversity, productivity, and excellent care that Doctor Forbes had seen on Sheikh Hamman's property. It was near the Siwan outpost of Abou Shrouf, a mineral spring with drinking water of such superb quality that it was bottled and sold all over Egypt. While Father Dave and others were swimming in pools below the Abou Shrouf spring, I went about inventorying a garden that had two understories of crops growing within waflelike hods beneath the shade of date palms.

It was a desert cornucopia. That first summer I visited Abou Shrouf I spotted dates and figs; pomegranates, peaches, and plums; olives and

Plates

All photographs are by Gary Paul Nabhan

Hopi terraced fields and orchards at Lower Moenkopi near Tuba City, Arizona, with an adobe-and-stone-walled pueblo in background.

Limestone-lined acequia, *irrigation ditch, in Diné orchards at Moenave, Arizona.*

Adobe-walled torreón, *tower, at the Roxanne Swentzell Tower Gallery. Part of the*
Poeh Cultural Center of the Pojoaque Pueblo in northern New Mexico.

(left) Remnant torreón *at the*
abandoned headquarters of the
Banu Nabhani in Oman.

Limestone-lined al-saqiyah *as part of the* falaj *or* qanat *irrigation system near Nizwa and Bahla, Oman.*

A traditional Berber meal at the Saharan (Libyan) Desert oasis of Siwa includes Old World and New World delicacies, such as chilis, lemons, fava bean puree, olives, and Jews mallow, as well as New World crops adopted by the Berbers.

An Omani protected-area ranger approaching a Boswellia sacra *tree that produces the frankincense formerly traded by the Banu Nabhani tribe over many centuries.*

An Alwad Ali Bedu nomad and his dromedary cross the gibbel plains of the Sahara (Libyan) Desert of western Egypt.

In downtown Beirut, Lebanon's first farmers market, Souk el-Tayeb, feature vendors such as "Mr. Pickles," Gerges Souaid, of Byblos. He offers many of the same home-processed pickles and jams as well as strings of fresh garlic that one might see in the U.S. Southwest.

(left) On a plateau above Bahla Fort, a World Heritage Site, lie several villages of Nabhan descendents who live in pueblo-like structures reminiscent of the U.S. Southwest.

The pastured slopes of limestone ridges near Kfar Zabad in the Bekaa Valley of Lebanon rise above fields of wheat and orchards of apricots and peaches; comparable landscapes can be found in southern Arizona and New Mexico.

(right) The wetlands of the Kfar Zabad hima, *or community-conserved wildlife refuge, in Lebanon contain many of the same plant species or genera found in* cienega *wetlands of the U.S.–Mexico borderlands, such as cattails (*Typha*), rushes (*Scirpus*), willows (*Salix*), poplars (*Populus*), and salt cedars (*Tamarix*).*

The astonishing diversity of wheat and barley breads baked by Walid Ataya of the Bread Republic in Beirut attests to the ancient culinary traditions still being celebrated in the Middle East.

Many of the herbs grown by this organic farmer from Lebanon have made their way to deserts of Mexico and the U.S. Southwest, where they are now featured in recipes derived from Arab, Jewish, and Moorish immigrants to the Americas.

This Bekaa Valley landscape—set beneath the snow-capped Mount Lebanon highlands—is part of the Fertile Crescent, one of desert agriculture's oldest and best-studied centers of origin.

okra; bananas and basil; grapes and Jews mallow; castor beans and squash. Two years later, when I came back to Abou Shrouf with world-renown garden photographer David Cavagnaro during the winter of Big Chill at dawn up in the dunes, I noticed guavas and henna, alfalfa and clover, onions and sugarcane. All told, a solitary Berber farmer at Abou Shrouf, Omar Ahmed Ali, was cultivating almost thirty crop species, both annual and perennial, in less than a hectare, an area smaller than most supermarket parking lots in the United States.

But what struck me the most about the Abou Shrouf garden was its resemblance to the Quitovac one that my old friend Luciano Noriega had cultivated for more than four decades in the Sonoran Desert. The hods or waffle grids were nearly the same size, and the dates, pomegranates, and figs nearly the same height. In both locations, they were placed on the borders of the grid, for they had better tolerance than vegetables do to the "bathtub ring" of salts deposited as soil crusts on the borders following each irrigation event. The vegetables down in the beds of the waffle grid were inundated with water and stayed "sweeter" beneath the trees than they would have if they had been exposed all day to direct sun; if they did not have their shady protection, the soil around the roots would look like the salty strip ringing a margarita glass.

By the end of my second visit there, I had confirmed that at least eighteen of the crop species that Doctor Forbes had recorded still persisted in the groves and gardens of Siwa. Siwans are very proud of the native (*baladi* or *bi-Siwi*) heirloom varieties of the twenty-seven crop species that have persisted there for hundreds of years. Some, such as the *saidi* date, the *hamed* olive, and the yellow-flowered *karkade* hibiscus tea, are considered among the most flavorful in all of Egypt and have international markets as well. It is curious that although, to my knowledge, none of the crop plants that Dr. Forbes introduced to Giza and Siwa has persisted, one ornamental cactus that he gifted to the sultan can still be seen in botanical gardens and in pots alongside hotel entranceways throughout Egypt. It is a miniature prickly pear that goes by the name *Opuntia microdasys*.

My only regret about going to Siwa when I did was that I had not done so while Miss Laura Kerman was still alive, for she would have been excited to hear about a place in a desert so distant from her own where Doctor Forbes had befriended Berbers and Bedouins, folks not unlike her own O'odham in sensibility. Unfortunately, in the last few years of her century-spanning life, she succumbed to a rather ironic form of senile dementia. When at last she was finally so feeble that she was taken from her father's house and placed in an urban nursing home, she could not remember the names of anyone still living or the consequences that led to her forced removal from the desert she loved. All she could remember— with perfect clarity—were events that had occurred in the desert long before the Great Depression, when she was in the service of Bonaventure Oblasser and of Doctor and Mrs. Forbes.

This selective memory caused me some embarrassment and sadness the last several times I went to visit Miss Kerman. She loved the cactus fruit, tepary beans, and creosote bush tea I brought her from the desert, but when I was with her, she simply could not remember for sure who I was. She seemed to feel comfortable with me, however, and spoke with affection to me in both O'odham and English, as if she were nevertheless certain that I was indeed someone who had earlier been part of her life. On one visit, she mistook me for a Franciscan brother who had worked with her and Father Bonaventure before World War II, teaching catechism to O'odham families on the other side of the border, not far from the oasis of Quitovac. On another, she watched me take my jacket and hat off—it had been a cold and blustery winter day in the Sonoran Desert— and then her expression grew intense as I presented her with a bundle of the desert's medicinal plants that she could ingest when the nurses weren't looking. She looked at me puzzled for a while and then suddenly smiled and said to me, "Well, then, how is Mrs. Forbes feeling today? Are her spirits any better?"

CHAPTER 5

That Cosmopolitan Look

The Plants That Make You Forget Your Country

I WAS BACK AT ABOU SHROUF, but running out of desert light. The sun was sinking behind one of a thousand dunes in sight, and I was having trouble finishing my work before darkness fell on the Sahara. I had just about completed an inventory of all the plants found around the spring-fed wetlands and the plantation of Omar Ahmed Ali when I came across one last fruit tree that I simply could not identify.

"Any idea what this kind of spiny shrub is over here?" I shouted over to David, who was barely in sight. I was calling out to David Cavagnaro, photographer, gardener, and insect ecologist with a near-photographic memory for the names of flowers and fruits. He had been busy taking one last photo on the other side of the orchard. When I looked his way, all I could see was his curly hair sticking up through some palm fronds. A few minutes later he came over to where I was standing next to the unidentified tree. He eyed its leaves, sought (without luck) any remnant flowers or fruit, then slowly shook his head.

"Looks familiar, doesn't it?" I beckoned.

"Sort of," he whispered. I surmised that he too was running through his mental hard drive, trying to narrow down the options.

"I know I've seen it somewhere before . . . out in the desert . . . in an oasis like this one," I offered, still bewildered.

"Here in Egypt?" David queried me.

"That's the trouble," I mumbled. "I've been to so many doggone oases in a mess of desert countries, they're all beginning to blur together."

David looked at me, bemused.

"Yep, too much time in the hot desert sun," I offered before David could kid me about it. "By now, I've probably burned out all brain cells suitable for storing botanical memories."

There is a kind of amnesia that can attack the minds of field naturalists when they are plopped into unfamiliar places. These naturalists see plants that seem vaguely familiar to them, but whose particular identities remain elusive, as if the plants' names and addresses are lodged in a little black book that cannot be immediately opened. This sort of amnesia has afflicted me several times, especially when I have moved back and forth between the desert oases of the Americas and those of the Middle East. During such moments, I sense that I know the plant in question from its growth form, color, vigor, and thorniness, but I cannot fully conjure up where and when I have met it before or what to call it.

This experience is much like the feeling I have when I am first introduced to distant relatives who have lived in Syria, Lebanon, Jordan, Egypt, or Oman all of their lives, but who look remarkably like cousins, aunts, and uncles whom I've known all my life in the Lebanese immigrant communities of America. A nappiness of hair, a lengthiness of nose, a puffiness of eyelids, a pudginess of hands, a frantic gesture or keening laughter are spooked with *familiarity*. These diagnostic traits tell me that someone is kin even though I don't know his or her name, profession, parentage, or pastime. ·

When it comes to keying out plants, I can often identify them to scientific family or genus, determine whether they are edible or poisonous, burnable or carveable, even when I don't actually know what they are named or from where they originally came.

This has been particularly true when I have had encounters with plants from desert oases, whether the oasis is situated in the Levant, on the Arabian Peninsula, on the Sinai, or within the Libyan Desert stretch of the Sahara.

Lately I've been nicknaming such nameless shrubs, trees, and herbs *the plants that make you forget your country*. I use this nickname especially in honor of three species of *Zizyphus* that have been associated with that phrase since the era when Homer compiled the *Odyssey*.

One of the three plant species is a grayish, thorny shrub known as the lote tree, *Zizyphus lotus*; it is the very same plant whose name eluded both me and David Cavagnaro during that Saharan sunset. The 1913 edition of *Webster's Revised Unabridged Dictionary* refers to its mythic history: "[It is] the lotus of the lotus-eaters, probably a tree found in Northern Africa, Sicily, Portugal and Spain (*Zizyphus lotus*), the fruit of which is mildly sweet. It was fabled [by Homer and others] to make strangers who ate it forget their native country, or lose all desire to return to it."

The second species capable of engendering such forgetfulness is known in English as the crown of thorns, *Zizyphus spina-Christi*. Yes, *the* crown of thorns, the one with branches so spiny and twisted that when reputedly placed on the head of Yeshua of Nazareth some two thousand years ago, nested firmly against his skull, it heightened his pain, causing bleeding and blackouts. When ethnobotanist Joseph Hobbs lived among the Ma'aza Bedouins in the Egyptian wilderness, he learned that they never cut the branches of this tree, for it is considered a sacred antiquity planted during the time of the Romans.

The third is the jujube, *Zizyphus jujuba*, with a waxy-looking but delicious fruit that can now be found around the world.

These shrubs may stick, prick, or prod you into forgetting, but they remain widely esteemed for certain other qualities and products they offer desert travelers. Consider a commentary written in 1935, when that renegade Victorian and reckless vagabond Freya Stark went off into the Arabian *deserta* where no other Western woman had ventured before. Arriving at the oasis of Ghayada in the frankincense-growing region of Yemen known as the Hadhramaut, Stark could see that "wide-spreading 'ilb or *nebk* trees (*Zizyphus spina-Christi*) stood before it [the oases]. After the palm, 'ilb is the most useful tree in the Hadhramaut. It needs no irrigation and grows in drier places, and provides food in its powdery apple-colored berries for the Bedouin, and fodder for their goats, and timber for all the carved doors and columns of the town."

Three-quarters of a century after Stark, the botanical Birchers—a father and daughter team that cataloged the useful plants of Egypt—recalled the mythic dimensions of the lote tree: "this species is said to be the genuine lotus of the ancient inhabitants of the Libyan coast, known as *Lothophages*. . . . In the Sudan, the dried and fermented pulp of its fruit is made into cakes [and] may have been the food of the Libyan Lothophagi mentioned by Pliny."

Abou Shrouf, that spring-fed oasis out in the Libyan Desert where David and I scratched our heads before the lote tree, may once have been inhabited by such Lotus-Eaters. I imagine them to be a forgetful and apolitical lot, caring little, over the centuries, whether their home place was recognized as part of Egypt (Misr) or Libya.

Perhaps they had eaten more than their fill of that fruit of forgetfulness.

What strikes me as paradoxical is that no one quite remembers where exactly these thorny members of the lote tree lot originated. Food historian Alan Davidson focuses on the jujube in the following commentary: "Whether it originated in China or Syria is not clear, but it is cultivated for its fruits right across this range: in Japan, China, Afghanistan, Iran, and westwards to the Mediterranean region."

And so we have a set of thorny shrubs in the genus *Zizyphus* for which no one really remembers their place of origin. They occur at desert oases all along the Frankincense Trail from the Hadhramaut region of Yemen clear to Damascus in Syria; across the Silk Road from Baghdad through Samarkand, Tashkent, and Karakul, clear to Kashgar and Canton in China; and across the western spice route from the souks along Alexandria's Lote Tree Lane through Abou Shrouf and Siwa in the Libyan Desert and on to Carthage and Fez.

Today, the jujube can be found in Tucson, Guaymas, San Diego, and Mexicali. All three lotus fruits have been carried by camel or horse across barren sands, to be planted wherever the salty soil was wet enough to embrace their roots. This process has occurred for so long that no one can discern where their natal grounds are located.

Hardy plants such as these serve as the masters of long-distance dispersal. These botanical hitchhikers have conned and connived caravans of dromedaries and Arabian steeds into carrying them along from oasis to oasis, with hundreds if not thousands of kilometers between one suitable habitat and the next. Because of this peculiar adaptation—of not really being native anywhere, but being at home nearly everywhere—lote trees are the perfect examples of what ecologists mean by the term *cosmopolitan species*. They are weedy and ready to ride along with any human gullible enough to serve as their agent of dispersal.

The lote trees thus tell us less about the past and a whole lot more about the future of our planet. As nature writer David Quammen has darkly prophesized, we have done our best to leave behind the Pleistocene as well as the Holocene in order to enter an era that will become known as the Homogecene.

In other words, we are rapidly turning this earth into the Planet of Weeds.

During the Homogecene, we may finally accomplish the task our species began to dedicate itself to some ten thousand years ago: of making each distinctive place on earth *more* like every other one until we no longer dwell in any particular place, only placeless space. This place is what has become known as the Geography of Nowhere.

Now there, you may be rebutting, the ubiquity of a few species of *Zizyphus* does not in and of itself make an instant Homogecene. Right you are, but I can only wish that the lote tree were the sole cosmopolitan species that "sleeps around," sleezing its way from one desert oasis to the next. It is simply not so, however.

Many plants other than those in the genus *Zizyphus* have found their way from one desert oasis to the next, from a desert on one continent to a desert on an altogether different one, and from one riverbank to another some ten thousand kilometers away.

Of the many great rivers that cross through the seas of sand scattered across this planet, I have had the good fortune to go weed hunting along two of the greatest, the River Nile and the Río Colorado. For the Nile, my family once boarded a felucca at Aswan and sailed with a bunch of Nubian Rastafarians for four days until we had had our fill of Bob Marley and the Wailers, carp, and couscous. For the Colorado, I have taken various trips down from its confluence with the Green, through Cataract Canyon; from there, southward through the now-inundated and dammed Glen Canyon; and, later, westward through nearly every stretch of the Grand Canyon, before skipping south a few stretches to witness its lowest reaches, down on the delta edging the Sea of Cortés.

The night before the felucca's launch near Aswan, I made the mistake of purchasing a rather expensive book entitled *The Weed Flora of Egypt* without peeking under its cellophane wrapper to peruse its contents. The following day, while sunning myself on the deck of the Nubians' felucca, I finally had a chance to inspect the innards of that pricey field guide.

I found, much to my dismay, that *I already knew* nearly every damned plant described in the entire volume because most of them grew on the Río Colorado as well! Some forty-one species of weeds that had spent millennia along the Nile had now found open ground on the banks of the Colorado. Likewise, at least five species from American deserta had made it to Egypt and bedded down on the shores of the Nile.

There on the deck of the felucca, I chanted out a litany of their names, like some old Catholic priest celebrating mass in Latin:

Oh, let us now praise the famous and ubiquitous weeds: *Amaranthus graecizans, Spergularia marina, Chenopodium album, Chenopodium ambrosioides, Chenopodium murale, Centaurea calcitrapa, Cichorium endive, Conyza aegyptica, Eclipta alba, Lactuca serriola, Matricaria chamomile, Silybum marianum, Sonchus asper, Sonchus oleraceus, Xanthium spinosum, Xanthium strumarium, Convolulus arvensis, Brassica nigra, Brassica tournefortii, Capsella bursa-pastoris, Sisymbrium irio, Euphorbia prostrata, Mentha longifolia, Alhagi maurorum, Medicago sativa, Melilotus indica, Malva parviflora, Oxalis corniculata, Argemone mexicana, Plantago major, Portulaca oleracea, Veronica anagallis-aquatica, Datura stramonium, Solanum nigrum, Urtica urens, Phyla nodiflora, Tamarix ramosissima, Avena fatua, Cynodon dactylon, Dactyloctenium aegyptium, Digitaria sanguinalis, Echinochloa colonum, Echinochloa crusgalli, Eleusine indica, Eragrostis cilianensis, Lolium perenne, Poa annua, Polypogon monspeliensis, Setaria glauca Setaria verticillata, Setaria viridis, Sorghum halepense.* And for dessert, a wild watermelon, *Citrullus lanatus.* Amen!

It might have been an ancient chant sung in Berber, Hebrew, or Arabic, for these species have been flexing their weediness for as long as humans have been plowing up the fertile earth of the Nilotic floodplain. Or perhaps for longer than that. As the felucca floated downstream and I scanned the floodplain's patchwork of vegetation, I realized that the Nilotic floods had been selecting disturbance-adapted plants long before the pharaoh's farmers came upon the scene. The Nile would surge during the flood season, then slowly recede to expose moist, fertile ground that was littered with seeds that dropped out of the floodwaters. The resulting seedlings had to get up into the light rather rapidly if they were to avoid being shaded out by their competitors, which could also suck the moisture dry beneath the reach of their roots. Long before Egyptians were intentionally cultivating crops on the Nile, it is likely they were harvesting those weedy plants that volunteered to cover the earth as the floodwaters receded. Jews mallow, purslane, chicory, and mustard were among those volunteers. They are eaten still today, for despite ten thousand years of Egyptians' picking them, they have never gone away.

Two decades ago a biological anthropologist named David Rindos suggested that such plants are essentially self-domesticating; that is, they have ecologically adapted to being productive in the habitats that are most frequently disturbed by humans, fires, and floods. Humans are just one more means for these plants to get their seeds dispersed. Such a notion has recently come into vogue, with our most eloquent science writers—from Michael Pollan to Jared Diamond—taking up its banner. Perhaps, they suggest, these plants have domesticated us and not the other way around.

As much as I love to ponder this curious and insightful inversion, I also shudder whenever I think of its ultimate consequences: a couple hundred species, such as tumbleweeds, have become so successful in associating themselves with human-modified landscapes that they have usurped the space, nutrients, and water once shared with tens of thousands of other plants. If humans have proved to be good at anything on earth, it is at *disturbing* things—that is to say, at *mucking things up*. Some 40 percent of the world's land surface has been modified to feed just one species, *our species*, by means of these disturbance-adapted associates. Decades after we abandon a place that our forefathers shaped, these cosmopolitan species persist, usually failing to welcome back the more geographically restricted natives that came before them.

If all we want of the earth is some space where we can be sheltered and fed so that we can have the energy and leisure to breed, then the self-domesticating, disturbance-adapted species are perfect means to that end. But there are reasons that the face of the earth should not be entirely made over in our own image, as Ceiridwen Terrill has recently offered in her fine book *Unnatural Landscapes*. For starters, such a makeover is not only rather boring, but also quite vain. It is the ecological equivalent of spending the entire day looking at ourselves in the mirror, as if our civilizations will never mature past the developmental stage of the hormonally impaired teenager.

I, for one—and perhaps you as well—adhere to the old maxim that *beauty is relief from monotony*. If all rivers are destined to be regulated by dams in a manner that makes their floodplain floras identical to those of the Nile and the Colorado, then we need fewer dams and more heterogeneity. We need more isolated oases free of the most ubiquitous of weeds. I can say it no better than Freya Stark did more than seven decades before I walked in her footsteps, as she passed through the southern gates of Arabia into an altogether refreshing desert landscape, rich in endemic plants and unique experiences: "If I were asked the most agreeable thing in life, I should say it is the pleasure of contrast. One cannot imagine anyone but an angel sitting with a harp in Paradise for ever. The ordinary human being needs a change. This is the secret charm of the oasis, usually an indifferent patch of greenery made precious solely by surrounding sands. The celebrated fountains of the world . . . all spring in arid places."

*II. Bridging Identities and
Family Histories in Two Worlds*

CHAPTER 6

A Desert Is a Home That Has Migrated

Our ancestors need to hear from us.
—Vivienne Jake, Kaibab Paiute elder

I. Late-Night News from Arabia

IT IS WELL AFTER MIDNIGHT, and I have found myself in the backseat of
a rented Lexus with a driver named Ahmed who is speeding at 150 kilometers per hour along the shores of the Arabian Gulf. There is desert here
right up to the sea, but I am having a hard time trying to make out what is
dry ground and what is ocean water. Floodlights beam down on the eight-
lane superhighway between Abu Dhabi and Dubai that obscure nearly
everything on either side of the pavement.

I spot an exit for a camel racetrack, but we do not take it. I catch
fleeting glimpses of Burger Kings, Subways, and Mall of America—all
nested in shopping centers not far off the freeway, but we pass them by.
The modernity and globalized glitz of the United Arab Emirates should
be overwhelming my spirit, but my soul has already wriggled loose of their
influence.

It has instead been roaming to the south and east, past the Empty
Quarter of the Arabian desert—the Rub al Khali—and into an era when
the Nabhani tribe of ahl-Hadr Arabs reigned over at least a five-hundred-
kilometer stretch of the Arabian Peninsula. Following the coast of the
Persian Gulf around the Straits of Hormuz, it comes to the core of their
territory, near the present-day Ṣuhar, Bahla, and Muscat in central
Oman. Back then, Bahla and Ṣuhar were capitals of a kingdom called
Nabhanid, one that gleaned copper from central Oman and precious
frankincense from the trees of southern Oman to send on their way west
to Ethiopia, Zanzibar, Egypt, and even Spain. Its port towns on the gulf
traded frankincense eastward across the Arabian Sea and Indian Ocean in
exchange for saffron, pepper, nutmeg, and cinnamon. Incense, fragrant

herbs, and precious metals were first taken by the earliest Arabian sea-farers to the Malabar coast of India.

By 750 CE, these seafaring Arabs made it all the way to China. And roughly one thousand years ago—around the beginning of the Nabhanid era—one Arab trader named Abdallah al Omani left the port of Ṣuhar to live in China during its Sung dynasty. When he died, he left behind a manuscript in Arabic regarding his adventures in the spice trade with China, one that makes Marco Polo's own efforts pale by comparison.

Aroused by the potent chemicals in those spices, my imagination has been racing back through the past millennium, wondering when, among those many centuries, the Banu Nabhani tribe had land to call their own, land in which their own spirits felt deeply rooted. Why, for other extended periods of time, did they live as rootless as tumbleweeds blown clear across the howling sands? Is my family's own heritage comparable to that of many refugees around the world in that we have abruptly (been) moved from place to place, never really becoming rooted anywhere for very long?

As the Lexus comes to a stop at the miragelike airport of Dubai, I make a pact with myself to track my father's family history down to the very ground from which it emerged. I decide to gather the answers to my questions in places such as Muscat, Bahla, Damascus, Byblos, and the Bekaa Valley. Like Dubai, many of these places have been radically trans-formed since the time the Nabhani last inhabited them. Old Dubai itself was first replaced by oil refineries, then by an instant metropolis plopped down in its midst. It now has million-dollar racetracks where camels once roamed on their own, unimpeded by tracks and bleachers. Such chimeri-cal images prompt me to recall an ancient aphorism frequently repeated among nomads of the Sahara: *a desert is a homeland that has migrated.*

Which has shifted more over the centuries? My father's clan, its values and dreams, or these sandy lands themselves, tortured by misuse, ex-hausted of their former fertility, blown away, paved over, and obscured?

"You can never go home again" may seem to be a peculiarly American take on the world, but is it accurate in a world where one out of every three people is from a family of political or economic refugees, either because their homeland is destroyed or because they cannot return to their place of birth at all? What is left out of this bald one-in-three statistic is the probability that many more of us are *ecological refugees*, forced to be weaned from our motherland because it has been ravaged by drought, locusts, fire, floods, typhoons, or our own taxing practices of poor soil and water management.

I mull over these possibilities not merely for those whose surname is the same as my own, but for Every Person and Every Habitat that is on the face of this earth. As so-called *Homo sapiens,* we have certainly never been as rooted as plants are in their habitats, but neither are we inexorably destined, like an HIV virus, to destroy fully our living habitat, our host. Can we find our ancestral home ground as Arthur Haley and many others have done, or has that ground already been swept out from under us?

Being somewhere between an ancient cactus and a deadly microbe in our lifestyles, however, gives us plenty of room to accumulate soil around our base or to blow it all away. And so my imagination races back through history, then forward again, as I decide how I will discern just exactly where my ancestors gravitated between these two poles.

Within another nine months, I am flying through Dubai once more— this time, across the northern reaches of the Empty Quarter—to Oman, where it appears that my ancestors spent more time than they have spent in any other landscape.

There, I hope to gauge their relative rootlessness by the stories told about them as well as by the stories they themselves have told. I close my eyes on the outskirts of modern Dubai and strain my ears to hear those stories as another Arab driver turns up the radio and floods the car with oud music that seems as ancient as any still made on earth. Somewhere in the droning sounds that accompany that oud's melody, I begin to hear my family's stories and perhaps some of yours as well . . .

II. Unscrambling Levantine Legacies

If you ask any of the cousins I grew up with about the origins of the Nabhan clan, they will immediately respond by saying that we have Lebanese (and perhaps Syrian) roots. But once I heard a Lebanese cousin who was showing me through the souks of Byblos speak with pride of our cultural heritage by claiming that we were direct descendants of the Phoenicians. Because his own immediate family lived near the most famous of the Phoenician ports, where he heard or saw something of its history every day, it was perhaps natural for him to claim that our ancestry was not desert Arab but coastal Phoenician—a name meaning "the people of the purple dye" because of the brilliant violet tints they once extracted from a shellfish akin to Mexico's *purpura panza*.

Rather than associating our heritage with camel caravans loaded with spices, he assumed that our ancestors were boat builders, navigators, and textile dyers as well as seafarers. As we looked out over the picturesque Phoenician harbor there, its colorful fish markets, antiquities shops, and sidewalk cafés, these claims seemed not only plausible but appealing. That is, why not celebrate with my cousin that our Nabhan contemporaries, like other Lebanese, must certainly share blood with those early Phoenicians who arrived in the eastern Mediterranean some five thousand years ago?

Those Lebanese who wish themselves to be pure-blooded Phoenicians should probably consider that over the past twelve centuries some fourteen different conquering forces went on the rampage in the Levantine interior, the countries now called Lebanon and Syria. They raped, pillaged, and plundered as they passed through, and they occasionally took wives (or husbands) from the local populace by legitimate means. If that is true, then how could it be that any Lebanese from the interior are pure-blooded Phoenicians at this late date?

For better or worse, most back-country Lebanese and Syrians are mutts. The five million Lebanese still living inside the Old Country are just as much mutts as the fifty million folks of Lebanese descent living beyond the Levant. Perhaps that's what we get for having ancestors that had a predilection for living around cultural crossroads and harbors. Miscegenation has been the norm, not the exception. This truth is not exclusive to the Lebanese; it likely describes the ancestry of many of you reading this history who identify with particular ethnicities.

III. Sedentary Arabs Who Moved Around

As many cultures—from Gypsies to Cherokees—have demonstrated, genetics may be one issue, but cultural identity is altogether different. In the Middle East, you can be a member of a clan or tribe by simply claiming (even by marriage) allegiance to a known common "ancestor." That allegiance has been historically demonstrated through a kindred or corporate spirit known as 'asabiyya. Genes don't matter as much as allegiances do.

The clan of my father's side of the family was historically known as the Nabahina or Banu Nabhani tribe, with the terms *nabahina* (collective plural) and *al-nabhani* (singular) originally meaning "outstanding" and "noble." They were one of the ahl-Hadr tribes of the Arabian Peninsula, not of the Mediterranean coast of the Levant. To be distinguished as one of the ahl-Hadr tribes historically meant that they were already "dwellers of fixed abodes," unlike the ahl-Bedu, or nomadic Bedouin.

Itinerant Bedu sheepherders still coexist with our kin in the Bekaa Valley of Lebanon today. They currently rent my cousins' mountain pastures and bring them *zaatar*-flavored yogurt and cheese fermented from the milk of ewes grazing on this wild thyme in the summer. Nabhans may live in close proximity to camel-caravaning Bedu, but we are not Bedu. In fact, my family has many of the agrarian biases against the nomadic life of the Bedu that are expressed in an eighth-century poem fragment from Bashār ibn Burd:

[My father] never had to sing a camel song
while trailing along behind such a scab-ridden beast,
nor did he ever resort to piercing tiny colocynths—
the wild watermelons—to quench his hunger & thirst,
neither did he have to knock down with a stick
the pods of native legume trees—mimosa, carob, acacia—
nor did we need to roast on meager coals
a skink while its tail still flailed & quivered
nor did I ever have to devour a desert lizard
that I dug with my own hands out of the stony ground.

There may be very good historical reasons why members of the Banu Nabhani tribe have exhibited a sense of place less like that of Bedu sheepherders and Phoenician seafarers and more like that of farmers of the Persian uplands, the floodplains of the Fertile Crescent, and the valleys draining out to the Arabian Sea along the coasts of Yemen and Oman. Along with the Hinawis, Aus, Khazras, and kindred Tayy, the Banu Nabhani tribe may have been among the original Arab populations of Yemen that later dispersed to many parts of the Arabian Peninsula, the Fertile Crescent, and beyond.

Their original dwelling place, according to the great historian of Arab peoples Albert Hourani, was "Yemen in south-western Arabia, a land of fertile mountain valleys and a point for long-distance trade. . . . The mountains of Yemen lie at the extreme point of an area touched by the monsoon winds of the Indian Ocean, and this is where regular cultivation of fruits and grains had long been carried on."

Sometime between when Yuhannis the Dipper and Yeshua of Nazareth were baptizing people in the River Jordan and when the Prophet Muhammad was sparking the fervor among newly converted Moslems, these original Arab tribes departed from Yemen to seek green pastures elsewhere. It appears that this dispersal was triggered by invasions from Ethiopia and by depletion of Yemen's agricultural productivity, culminating in the sixth century CE with the destruction of the Marib dam and the tens of thousands of hectares that it formerly irrigated.

Although these southern Arab peoples had traveled north in earlier centuries and were known as far north as present-day Baghdad in the sixth century BCE, they were now looking to settle permanently in the more arid reaches of the Arabian Peninsula and the Fertile Crescent.

Most of the Banu Nabhani tribal members went northeastward toward the Straits of Hormuz, but others did not necessarily pass in the same direction. At the least, they quickly moved on from Oman, perhaps following an old camel route from Liwa in the north or from al-Baleed in the south that crossed the Empty Quarter to Yabrin, then curved southeastward to Mecca or Medina. Early in the Christian era, some of the Banu Nabhani and their Tayy kinsmen ended up on the western coast of the Arabian Peninsula; in fact, the Tayys had more or less become a subtribe of the Banu Nabhani there. It is likely that many of the Banu Nabhani may have been Christianized Arabs by this time, but continued to have close social and economic ties with Omani and Yemeni Jews. What we know from a rather infamous incident is that they did not always marry among the same people or keep the same religion as before.

In one multicultural community of this era, a Nabhan man fell in love with a Jewish girl from the Hebrew-speaking Banu al-Nadir tribe. This couple spawned a child named K'ab b Ashraf, who loved to play with words. He became a well-known poet, and because he was raised as a devout Jew, he was nicknamed al-Nadir to draw attention to his mother's ancestry.

Unfortunately, al-Nadir's playfulness with words, in particular his capacity for parody and satire, did not go over so well with everyone. In one public performance, his poems poked fun at a certain Muhammad, who was the recipient of an altogether new prophesy. Muhammad was apparently not amused by these jokes and ordered his newly converted followers to assassinate al-Nadir.

To this day, a debate rages among both Moslems and Jews regarding Muhammad's insistence that this nonbeliever be assassinated. Had the order been given because K'ab b Ashraf al-Nadir ibn Banu Nabhani was deeply disrespectful with his words or because he adhered to Jewish thought and custom? There are those who maintain that the soon-to-be Prophet Muhammad, after some frustrating experiences while running spice trade caravans to Jerusalem and Basra for his first wife, was never again comfortable with Jews. They read into the assassination order a hatred for all Jews, not just for one satirist who was both Jewish and Arab by descent.

This watershed in history may have led to the ambivalence that some members of the Banu Nabhani have had regarding fervent religious devotion. It may have also made some Moslems wary of engaging with any quick-witted character who had the surname Nabhan. Who knows if it discouraged further pairings of al-Nabhanis with Jews for fear of producing another loose-tongued, politically inappropriate poet into the world?

With the coming of Yeshua of Nazareth, the fall of the Temple in Jerusalem, and the religious devotion fired up by the Prophet Muhammad, Banu Nabhani tribal values no doubt underwent dramatic transitions: allegiances and alliances shifted, and much of the tribe went on the move toward the eastern stretches of the Arabian Peninsula. Following the Hijrah migration of Muhammad's kinfolk to found and spread Islam as a way of life, an era of rootlessness rather than rootedness prevailed across the region. By the ninth century, so many skirmishes had occurred among displaced tribes that the resulting political chaos had created a state of anarchy from Oman south of the Straits of Hormuz to Basra at the northern tip of the Persian Gulf.

It was during this chaotic period—between 908 and 931 CE—that the Abbasid caliphate finally lost much of the control and tax base that it had earlier gained across the entire region. In essence, there was suddenly a complete deterioration of the feeling of unity in the Moslem world that had coalesced by having a single sovereign for all tribes over the previous two centuries. Taking advantage of this hiatus in political unity, the incorrigible Muhammad bin Nur wreaked havoc over much of the Arabian Peninsula. In his 1928 classic *The Persian Gulf*, Sir Arnold Talbot Wilson suggests why the tribes of the peninsula were ready for fresh leadership that would be capable of dealing with Muhammad's bad behavior: "He cut off the hands and ears, and scooped out the eyeballs of nobles, inflicted unheard-of outrages upon the inhabitants, destroyed watercourses, burnt the books, and utterly destroyed the country."

At last, Muhammad bin Nur's tyranny was met with "the wrath of an infuriated people," whose tribes disposed of his deputies, but then kept quarreling among themselves. This power struggle worsened when the last imam, Jaber Moussa bin Abi Al Maali Moussa bin Nejad, died in 1154 CE; then, as White suggests, "a Nabhan tribe acquired ascendancy and ruled until the reestablishment of the Imamate," an event now dated at roughly 1500 CE, around the time of Portuguese arrival on the west coast of Arabia. Wilson was able to trace the influence of this tribe in the southeastern corner of the Arabian Peninsula until 1624 CE. The length of this influence may suggest that my Nabhan kin had at last found a home in which some of them developed an enduring sense of place. As Arab historian Hourani has noted, they had found a home in Oman not dissimilar to their earlier one in Yemen.

IV. The Ancient Motherland We Had Forgotten

Today, as I amble among the piñon trees and sumac shrubs above my home in Arizona, I carry with me a walking stick given to me by Ali Masoud Al-Subhi, an Omani agricultural scientist from the oasis of Nizwa. He carved it out of a sturdy branch of wild olive, taken from the slopes of Jebel al-Akhdar, a mountain range that has formed the core of the Nabhan homeland for more than a thousand years. The walking stick is shaped like a shepherd's staff and has been sanded and polished to a smoothness unlike any other wooden talisman in my possession. When I touch it, I am reminded of the first time I saw wild olives growing scattered along the limestone ridges of Jebel al-Akhdar, for those ridges look very much like the ones in the Bekaa Valley where most of my cousins live in Lebanon, as well as like the ones near where I've lived in Tucson and Flagstaff, Arizona. I have wondered whether preference for a certain kind of austere and arid landscape has embedded itself in my family's genes, so that, once displaced, we wander around until we find another that fits that same image in shape, color, and texture.

Ali once took me to a place just a few kilometers from his home in Nizwa, a place built almost a millennium ago, but now lying in ruin. It still had two-story dwellings of mud bricks poking up out of the rubble and was snuggled up against a limestone ridge that rose from the valley floor clear to the heights of Jebel al-Akhdar.

"Here is a blace your ancestors may have lived," Ali said matter-of-factly. "For certain, it was a village that the Banu Nabhani built during the beriod in which they were in bower."

I stepped out into the midday heat and scanned a few hundred meters of rubble that once housed several hundred people. I was stunned by the similarity between this village and the one where my grandfather was born in the Bekaa, called Kfar Zabad. In both cases, the little settlement sat just below a formidably steep slope of sheer limestone, one that absorbed the sun's heat as if it were the village solar collector. The similar positions in which these villages were situated relative to the mountains above them struck me as more than mere coincidence.

When I stepped back into the Land Cruiser where Ali had been waiting, rewinding his head scarf and cleaning his eyeglasses, I thanked him for bringing me there.

"I am grateful to you, Ali, for remembering this place as our home."

As someone who had lived most of his life within ten kilometers of these ruins, Ali must have taken my comment as a peculiar non sequitur, the kind that Americans seem habitually capable of making. He politely changed the subject.

"Let me show you something alive now, something that goes all the way back to the Nabhanid times," Ali said as we drove into the heart of Nizwa. "Do you know what *falaj* is? Earlier, you ask about *qanat*. That is Farsi word. Falaj is something like qanat."

We walked down to an ancient irrigation canal that ran into date groves downstream from where we stood. We slowly followed the meandering canal upstream, first to a wider pool where residents could cleanse themselves before prayer and then, farther up, to a place off-limits to bathing, where residents could draw water for drinking. And then, even farther upstream, the canal "went underground," which is to say that it was covered—like a horizontal well—for several hundred meters.

We could not see beyond this covered section, but Ali assured me that the water came from the mountains nearby, where several vertical shafts caught rain and runoff during storms and funneled this harvested water into the canal we saw at our feet.

"This falaj system still works, feeding dozens of gardens and date groves for the next several kilometers. Everybody helbs maintain the canals, and they ration water during drought. But even during drought, the falaj has hardly ever gone dry over the centuries since your tribe has lived in this area."

We wandered downstream, through one date grove after another, seeing how the canal wove through their midst, irrigating not only dates, but mangos, limes, sugarcane, melons, bananas, and maize as well. I later learned that one of the most delectable dates found in the Nizwa groves is called Qash Nabhani, a seedling palm named after the Banu Nabhani of the area. It is a big, soft, lentil-colored date, with thick white flesh that has a streak of gold running through it. Compared to the hundreds of other date varieties grown in Oman, this seedling date is rather rare, being known from only four villages, including Nizwa and nearby Samail. Those who regularly eat it say that the Qash Nabhani is not overbearingly sweet, but absolutely delicious, especially when it reaches the *tamr* stage of full maturity. Indeed, the dates of Samail are renowned through Oman and were once exported to other parts of the world, including Palm Springs, California.

From Nizwa, Ali took me to nearby Bahla, where a fortress begun in pre-Islamic times was rebuilt by the Banu Nabhani to serve as one of the capitals of their kingdom. From where we first caught a full view of Bahla, its ancient stone tower rose some sixty-five meters above the tallest palms in the date groves below. A mud-and-brick wall runs twelve kilometers around the date plantations, homes, shops, and souk marketplaces of the Bahla oasis.

Because of enduring living traditions like the falaj and pottery making, as much as for being what has been called "one of the most majestic monuments in all of Oman," Bahla is now recognized as a World Heritage Site by the United Nations. We could see the scaffolding along its walls where the United Nations Educational, Scientific, and Cultural Organization was assisting in the restoration of this monument as part of the effort to interpret the historic legacy of the Banu Nabhan tribe.

Bahla may be the place where the tribe became politically prominent, establishing the first capital of the Nabhanid kingdom there, but, according to Omanis, it is the mountains high above Bahla where the Nabhans have the longest continuous association.

Ali and I drove up the long and winding road that peaks out atop Jebel al-Akhdar. There he pointed out the wild olive trees that took root amidst the limestone slickrock, the same wild olives that he used to carve the walking stick for me.

"Maybe three-quarters of the beoble who live ub here are of the Banu Nabhani. I don't think you can meet them all in one day or even one week," Ali said, smirking. "You will need to come back and stay ub here or near us in Nizwa for several weeks if you are to get to know all of your relatives."

Within an hour of beginning our climb, we had reached two thousand meters above the seacoast where we had begun our day's journey. We had little time—not enough to visit all the villages on Jebel al-Akhdar—so Ali took me to two that had ancient terrace agriculture cascading down the mountainsides like so many verdant stair steps, similar to those that cover the rugged slopes of Yemen. At Wadi L'Ayn and Sheraga, I saw many of the same fruits and nuts in cultivation that my grandfather had first grown in Lebanon and then later hawked as an itinerant fruit peddler in the U.S. Midwest. There were apricots and peaches, pomegranates and almonds, melons and limes. There were pistachios and papayas, garlic and onions, spinach and radishes. But out of all this abundance, two of the cultivated plant traditions of Wadi L'Ayn pulled at my heartstrings.

The Nabhans and their neighbors there were growing prickly pears, one thorny wild type (*Opuntia humifusa*) and one spineless cultivar—no doubt *Opuntia ficus-indica*—from the deserts of Mexico or the U.S. Southwest. They looked much like cactus varieties I myself had grown for years in the Sonoran Desert of southern Arizona, with lusciously ripe crimson and violet fruit. How had these cacti gotten to the interior of Oman?

The other plant that instantly triggered memories was an exceedingly thorny rose, cultivated in extremely high densities for its flower petals. The hand-picked petals were used to concoct rose water, which was bottled locally and sold for rather high prices in the local souk. When I opened a bottle that one bazaar shopkeeper handed me, I was overwhelmed by the fragrance, the same fragrance emanating from my grandfather's face whenever he kissed me, a curly-haired four-year-old at the time. There is no smell that I have associated more with the men who immigrated from the Old Country to America than that one.

V. The Heyday of Arabic Decadence

Perhaps because of some deeply embedded wanderlust, some members of the Banu Nabhani have always had a stronger inclination for cross-cultural and transoceanic trade than for the farming and crafts that occupied their kin in the mountains. During the Nabhanid era in Oman, they moved to the coast of the Arabian Sea at Liwa and Ṣuhar and established their second capital as a fortress amidst a pre-Islamic souk. When Portuguese seafarer Alfonso de Alburquerque first encountered the second Nabhanid castle in Ṣuhar in 1507, he found that it "was a fortress square in shape, with six towers around it, having over its gate another two very large towers."

The Ṣuhar fort was large enough to hold a thousand men and all their provisions comfortably. Five centuries later, when I visited the fort with my friend Sulaiman al-Khanjari, it seemed a bit less imposing, for the sea walls that enclosed the harbor some two hundred meters in front of it had washed away, leaving it more open and vulnerable. Bougainvilleas trailed over its ancient stuccoed walls, giving it more of the feel of a beach resort in the Mediterranean or the Yucatán.

However imposing the Ṣuhar fortress may have been, the historic importance of the Ṣuhar harbor itself cannot be underestimated. From it, early Arabic sailing dhows went up the Arabian coast to Basra to trade with people in present-day Iraq; they were soon crossing the Straits of Hormuz to Bandar Abbas in present-day Iran and to the Malabar coast, near present-day Karachi, India. The sheikhs of Ṣuhar—including Nabhan ibn Kuhlan, who began his reign in 1261, and Abu Muhammad ibn Nabhan, who lorded over much of Oman around 1330—had plenty of economic incentives for keeping these trade routes under their control.

In particular, they held onto trade from the interior hinterlands of the southerly, sparsely populated Dhofar region, where the *jeballi* mountain people harvested one of the world's most valuable products of their era, frankincense. Although the aromatic, milky-looking frankincense gum resins from several related trees are known as *lubán* (milk) in Arabic, the Dhofar frankincense, called *hojari*, is clear as a prism and worth more than any other in the world. From their homeland in the Dhofar province, the jeballi would haul loads of frankincense northward either by camel caravans or by dhows sailing out of the ancient port of al-Baleed. In either case, this sacred incense and medicine would make its way to Şuhar, where, along with copper, dates, wild thyme, and dry limes, it would be shipped out to trade for other spices from distant lands.

The Banu Nabhani were undoubtedly among the coastal Arabs who cornered the market on the northeastward trade of frankincense both by sea and by land. Although a safer frankincense trail left the Hadhramaut area of Yemen, passed eastward to San'a, then northward to Mecca, Medina, Petra, and Jerusalem, the Banu Nabhani likely controlled the more difficult overland route from Şuhar and Liwa to the Yabrin oasis, then northward to Bahrain, Baghdad, or Damascus.

From 1150 CE—when a few al-Nabhani traders first brought economic unity to the region—the Şuhar and Bahla fortresses were used by a long chain of Nabhan rulers who maintained a political and commercial dynasty *for a period longer than the present U.S. government has persisted in North America.* Muhammed al-Fallah may have been the first Banu Nabhan of that dynasty, emerging as a leader to be reckoned with by 1151, solidifying his power base by 1154, and prevailing until 1176. Nearly two dozen of the sequentially chosen individuals from the Banu Nabhani presided over a collective of cousins that dominated the secular, economic, and military affairs of various interior and coastal regions of Oman for the next five centuries.

Curiously, the Banu Nabhani influence eclipsed even that of the imams who had earlier been granted spiritual authority over the region. Even though Islam had been introduced to Oman around 630 CE, Oman's pivotal location in intercontinental commerce meant that the elected theocracy of the imamate did not preside over all its affairs. That commerce could remain in Omani hands only if there were leaders who maintained good diplomatic relations with surrounding nations, with neighboring tribes, and among themselves.

It appears that the Banu Nabhani were adept at maintaining trade relations with Persians, Hindis, and Africans, from Ethiopia all the way down past the Horn and in Madagascar; in fact, there are records of Nabhani rulers personally traveling to Ethiopia, Zanzibar, the Lamu Archipelago of present-day Kenya, and Persia. What they were far worse at was dealing with the bickering among local tribes and in quelling the struggles among themselves.

I winced and then chuckled when I read what the "official book" of Oman's history by the Omani minister of information had to say about my ancestors. Called *Oman in History*, it uses few kind words in its description of this motley crew of poet-kings, party animals, marauders, and extravagant consumers: "The Nabhans led lives of decadent luxury, and built citadels and fortifications to ward off the threats of their rivals . . . [but still] fought among themselves."

For most everyone else besides the ruling family, the minister concedes, "life in this era was grim." It was so grim that one frustrated heir to the Nabhan family fortune—Sultan Ahmad Abubaker Nabhan of the fourteenth century—absconded with some of his inheritance and established his own more idyllic kingdom, called Akhbar Pate, in the Lamu archipelago off the coast of Kenya.

I once met a Kenyan who had grown up on the biggest island of Lamu. "It's not only beautiful there, but history—archaeology if you will—is all around you. How do you know of Lamu? Most white Americans have never heard of us!"

When I told him of my family's historic connection to his birthplace, he burst out laughing, "I never thought I would meet an American who would admit that his 'roots' are entangled with my own!"

While members of the Banu Nabhani were off partying, irritating the most devout of their neighbors, and fighting among themselves, a previously unknown adversary surreptitiously arrived on the scene around 1498. In 1500, the Portuguese began to negotiate with those dissatisfied with the rule of poet-king Sulayman bin Sulayman Al Nabhan, the last Banu Nabhan ruler of all of Oman. That same year the Nabhanid dynasty collapsed, and Imam Muhammad bin Ismael was charged with cleaning up the mess that the Nabhans had left in their wake.

However, within a year's time, Portuguese seafarers captured the port of Muscat, then Ṣuhar, and all other major Omani ports, and soon had control of all other trade along the coast of the Arabian sea. If the Portuguese had first appeared to the Banu Nabhani like newcomers who were willing to trade valuable goods for exotic spices, within a short time it became painfully clear that they had come to lock up the spice trade between the Far East, Europe, and Africa. Most of the Banu Nabhani tribe fled to the interior at Jebel al-Akhdar, although a few remained involved in camel caravan trade at Ṣuhar and Liwa.

Perhaps their reign could not have lasted much longer anyway: the Banu Nabhani had been holding pivotal positions linking spice trade between Asia, Africa, and Europe for centuries. Now that sizeable Portuguese and Spanish ships had found ways to reach India and the East Indies on their own, the volume of spices carried by camel caravans across the Arabian Peninsula would seem miniscule by comparison.

From 1508 to 1617, the Portuguese gradually gained control over all the port towns in what is now Oman, the United Arab Emirates, and Bahrain, forcing the previously ruling tribes inland or away from their homelands altogether. A second, weaker era of Nabhanid rule, from 1508 to 1624, took place away from the coast, where the tribe still maintained control of the Bahla fortress and could escape to refuges in the rugged hinterlands of Jebel al-Akhdar if they needed to. Significantly, however, the Portuguese themselves did not venture into the interior, nor did they learn the sources of the hojari frankincense and copper. It appeared that both the fallen Nabhans and the indomitable jeballi tribesmen could survive if they kept to the interior, and they have done so to this day. But the Portuguese, by controlling all trade across the sea, usurped many of the Nabhans' former sources of income. These foreigners restructured the Omani economy until the Yaraʿriba (Yarubid) Arab tribes poured in from all sides to break their dominance.

Beginning around 1586 and continuing through 1650, the Yarubids ousted all Portuguese sailors, traders, and soldiers from the Omani coast. When they had finally accomplished their task, it was their tribes' Sultan ibn Sayf rather than a Nabhan who presided over the region. The Yarubids reestablished the imamate's political and spiritual control, but it was short-lived, for soon the Ottomans came in from the north and incorporated the region's economy into their vast empire. In the meantime, the Nabhans had only their empty fortresses and palaces to remind them of their former glory because they no longer had the resources to maintain their luxurious lifestyles.

The sobering summary of the Nabhanid dynasty issued by the Omani minister of information may apply not only to my family, but to any political power—from Saddam Hussein and the shah of Iran to George W. Bush—that has worn out its welcome within its own homeland:

The Nabhani Age, called so because their rule spanned five centuries, has been considered by the majority of historians as an age of . . . injustice, as they violated their subjects' rights. Modern historians employing a neutral scientific approach do not accept all of these facts as truths, as they lack serious scientific credibility. . . . The Nabhani age has [also] been described as an age of tyranny. However, there is not much difference between those mighty kings called tyrants by some Omani scholars, and the legitimately elected Imams. These statements should not be taken as self-evident truths. Just as there are good rulers, there are also corrupt rulers, and this applies to the Banu Nabhan.

VI. On the Road Again

From stories included in *One Thousand and One Arabian Nights*, we know that the fame and influence of the Banu Nabhani extended far beyond their homeland. By the twelfth century CE, the Banu Nabhani and their Tayy tribal affiliates had become widely traveled and welcomed by others in distant lands, but their good fortune made some of their hosts jealous as well. In one story in the *Arabian Nights*, a beautiful young woman from Baghdad is besieged by suitors, including a Nabhan sheikh, who arrives from the south via Mosul. To win her hand in marriage, this sheikh from the south comes to her with "great company," bringing her modest enticements: "a hundred she-camels laden with musk and lign-aloes and ambergris; and five score [camels more] loaded with camphor and jewels; and another hundred, laden with silver monies; and yet another hundred, loaded with raiments of silken stuffs, sendel and brocade; besides a hundred slave girls; and a century of choice steeds of swift and generous breeds."

Of course, no well-groomed girl from a sophisticated city in the north would ever fall for such cheap tricks from the south, so she promptly dismisses the Nabhan suitor!

In a story said to be first told on the 625th Arabian night, another unsuitable Nabhan—as wealthy and as tedious as a nouveau-riche Texas oilman—determined to wed a Baghdad beauty named Mahdiyah: "When Al-Haml, lord of the Banu Nabhan, heard of her charms . . . he took off on horseback with five hundred of his men to demand her hand."

Al-Haml's offer of marriage is also spurned, so he kidnaps Mahdiyah and her slave girls, only to have Baghdad's own Gharib the Stranger drive a lance through his heart and cut off his head. Gharib is so proud of his success in routing a "southerner" from the Arabian Peninsula that he composes this couplet on the spot: "I am he who is known on the day of the fight, / and the Jinn of the Earth at my shadow take flight!"

Fortunately, not all of the Nabhan and Tayy tribal members faired so poorly when they visited distant lands. In fact, some of the Tayy subtribe permanently moved to Baghdad, perhaps to promote their trade in frankincense and spices. Later they ventured even farther, into Central Asia, where they reputedly fell among the ranks of Arab-speaking merchants who sought goods brought from China by Silk Road caravans. After a while, all Arab-speaking traders in Farsi-dominated dialect areas were called "Tayys," for short, and, later, "Tajiks."

Some scholars claim that this is the origin of the name Tajikistan, signifying that it was a place of exchange along the Silk Road for Arabic-, Farsi-, and Mongolian-speaking traders. There remains in Tajikistan today a truly Arab enclave of traders, who use as their base the town of Shaartuz, not far from the Iranian border. The lessons learned in managing trade along the Frankincense Trail had apparently also had some value on the Silk Road, the other route that linked the caravans of the East with those of the West.

The Banu Nabhani tribe was no longer at the pinnacle of its political power on the Arabian Peninsula, but that did not mean that all Nabhans emigrated from the region, losing their centuries-old sense of place. I share my surname with hundreds of families who live near Ṣuhar and Liwa, Bahla and Nizwa. They can still trace their descent back through some twenty-two generations of affiliated tribes now called the Bani Riyam, which formerly received strong leadership from the Nabahina sheikhs. Nonetheless, we can be sure that more Nabhans did begin to wander beyond their homelands of the eastern Arabian Peninsula with the end of their dynasty in Oman.

VII. Westward to Lebanon and Beyond

What happened next to my direct Banu Nabhani ancestors remains obscure, but oral history among the family remaining in the Bekaa Valley of Lebanon suggests that they migrated first to Palestine. A Moslem teacher and judge born in 1849, Imam al-Qadi Yusuf al-Nabhani, had this to say about his family origins: "We go back to the Banu Nabhani, an Arab desert folk who settled of old in the village of Izjim. [It is] north of the Holy Sites in the land of Palestine, presently part of the district of Haifa in Akka, a province of Beirut."

From his own knowledge of family oral history, he traced his family in Izjim back four generations before his own, suggesting that they may have arrived from "the desert" in the area of Haifa between 1680 and 1740. Later, at least one branch of the westward-moving Banu Nabhan moved up to Mount Hauran, an area just forty kilometers south of Damascus near the border between Syria, Jordan, and Lebanon.

Mount Hauran is a forbidding, nearly treeless basaltic massif, with little livestock forage to offer in most years and few microhabitats suited to the cultivation of dates or field crops. It stands in stark contrast to the verdure of the home places the Banu Nabhani tribe had known in Yemen and Oman. It may be good for building stamina and spiritual rigor—and good for hunting chukar today—but it is unproductive relative to the oases and harbors that formerly offered the Nabhans their sustenance. Perhaps because of these features, Nabhan emigrants could more easily take refuge there without infringing upon the more productive territories of neighboring tribes. Perhaps they could escape religious persecution there or easily trade the wild anise seed that naturally sprouts and grows in years with adequate rainfall. But, in the end, Mount Hauran was perhaps more of a stopover for the tribe than a home with long-term potential.

The next time my Nabhan ancestors are recorded in history is from the Ras el-Metn area of Mount Lebanon, between the coast and the Bekaa Valley. There they formed alliances through marriage with the Abou Rjeily family, Christians who had also lived around Mount Hauran in the seventh century, where they had resisted conversion to Islam. The Abou Rjeilys had at some time moved from Mount Hauran to the seaport of Batroun north of Beirut, but left it as well.

Not long after dwelling on the coast, the Abou Rjeilys found suitable home ground in a mountain village of Druze and Christians below the summit of Ras el-Metn, sometime around the beginning of the seventeenth century, probably well before the first Nabhans moved there. Within a matter of decades, they, like others of Mount Lebanon, became involved in tending mulberry trees for silk production.

But like any family tree, the branches of ours cross with those of many others. If the Abou Rjeilys spent considerable time around Batroun on the coast, did they intermarry with the presumed descendants of the seafaring Phoenicians? Even though a core group of the Nabhans once came westward from Oman, do their centuries of intermarriage with Abou Rjeilys open up other issues regarding their ancestry?

They certainly do. For starters, although it appears that the Abou Rjeilys were steadfast Christians, it is not so clear that the Nabhans were as tenacious in adhering to just one religion. We know that some Nabhans were Maronite Christians who married Druze and that one branch of the family to arrive in Lebanon was made up of Sunni Moslems.

The word *Sunni* comes from the term *ahl al-sunnuh wal-jama'ah*, meaning "people of custom and community," who humbly attempt to mirror the Prophet's most admirable and devout behaviors in their own actions. Although my Nabhan ancestors may have been Christians prior to the emergence of Islam late in the sixth century, nearly every community on the Arabian Peninsula converted to Islam within a century and a half after the Prophet's death. Of course, some Nabhans may have held out as Christians, as the Abou Rjeilys did near Mount Hauran in Syria. But a return to Christianity for some Sunni Nabhans is just as likely and probably occurred within the past three centuries, after they had moved to Jordan, Syria, and Lebanon from the south and east of the Arabian Peninsula.

Ras el-Metn—Sheep's Head Mountain—is a place I have seen only from some distance because our cousins did not want me to get caught up in roadblocks maintained by Druze militiamen. But what I remember is looking out from a high ridge that was already dusted with snow to an even higher mass, kilometers away, that dwarfed anything else in the landscape. I had on a wool sweater, wool hat, and windbreaker, but I was still cold; I could only wonder what anyone living near Ras el-Metn was enduring if they too were outside at that particular moment.

What relatives have recalled to me, however, is that Ras el-Metn is a place of heavenly summers. During the era in which the Nabhan family still lived around the mountain in any number, it was thick with mulberry trees whose leaves were harvested for feeding to silkworms. At the time I heard these stories, I had no idea that silkworms had played a key role in triggering the Lebanese diaspora. After decade of converting their fields and orchards to mulberry plantations used to feed silkworms, the Mount Lebanon communities such as Ras el-Metn were cut off from the French silk buyers by the Turks just before World War I. With no market for their silk and little land left available for sowing grains and vegetables, the Lebanese families in the mountains were forced to abandon their homes. Many first fled to Beirut or to the Bekaa Valley, but, ultimately, hundreds of thousands emigrated to Europe, the Americas, and Australia. It was during the collapse of the silk industry that the Nabhans moved on for one last migration across the Middle East.

Fortunately, the family's more recent roamings are traceable through oral histories from the past two and a half centuries. These histories have the Abou Rjeily family as a focal point as much as the Nabhan family. One story involves a rather wayward Abou Rjeily named Elias from Ras el-Metn. Under circumstances surrounding a murder, he was forced to leave the mountains for the Bekaa Valley, settling first near the city of Zahle and then around the monumental ruins of Baalbek early in the nineteenth century. There he ran into Metri Nabhan, also of Ras el-Metn, who himself had fled after being accused of a murder. They serendipitously arrived in the valley just as Sunnis and Christians began to battle against the Druze family known as the Junblati in an attempt to expel them from the Bekaa. Through Elias, the militia of Prince Bashir el-Chehabi enlisted Abou Rjeily and Nabhan family members from the mountains to help them.

When the prince's Sunni and Christian forces won the battle in 1824, he seized all of the Junblati lands and offered them to his supporters. Metri Nabhan and Elias Abou Rjeily were offered land to farm that had been abandoned by the Druze. They were also invited by the Sunni to settle in a side canyon called Kfar Zabad, hidden off from the road between Zahle and Aanjar. They agreed to do so if their relatives from Ras el-Metn could come as well, for the Druze were regrouping there. Down in the valley, Elias's family decided to go by the name of Bourjaily.

It was in this manner that Metri Nabhan and Elias Bourjaily became the modern founders of the village community of Kfar Zabad into which my grandparents were born. Their descendants in the Bekaa became orchard keepers, wine makers, butchers, merchants, engineers, architects, herders, and *araq* distillers. The araq bootleggers had wonderful grapes in Kfar Zabad, but still returned to their ancestral homelands at

Mount Houran near the Syrian border every year to get the best anise seed to flavor their araq. There in the Bekaa, the Nabhans and Bourjailys have continued to intermarry to the present day.

Why did so many Nabhans and Bourjailys leave the Bekaa Valley for the Americas around the turn of the twentieth century? The Turks had taken over much of Greater Syria (including Lebanon) during the Ottoman War, forcibly conscripting tens of thousands of Lebanese men into their army to fight against other Arabs. Most of these men deserted and fled, but many were killed.

To make matters worse, a terrible drought and locust plague hit the region in 1912 soon after the silk industry collapse that had occurred at the beginning of the twentieth century. Thousands of families in the Bekaa were left on the brink of starvation and had to leave their land behind. But conditions were no better in Beirut, where many homeless women were forced to work as prostitutes, and dead bodies were piled high on the edges of the streets. American Protestant organizations helped these refugees board ships bound for Boston and New York. Many of their relatives soon attempted to follow on their own. Some bought cheap tickets for ships to "America," for them meaning the United States, but found themselves landing in Veracruz or Merida, Mexico, or in Brazilian ports instead.

As World War I began, much of the Bekaa Valley was depopulated. By the time Lawrence of Arabia and his Arab allies freed Damascus of the Turks, the valley's population was perhaps only one-twentieth of what it had been twenty-five years earlier. The French and English then set up their separate protectorates for Lebanon and Syria, respectively, leading to a far greater influence of French culture among most Nabhans.

Until I understood these historic facts, I had always been a bit ashamed that my forefathers left Lebanon. But their home had become a political and economic desert, and migration appeared to be their only possible salvation. Who can blame someone for attempting to escape from war, disease, pestilence, drought, and the collapse of a supporting industry?

According to Ellis Island records, twenty-six-year-old Petros Nabhan was the first of the family to emigrate to the United States, in 1893. Immigration of Nabhan clan members from the Old Country to America peaked between 1906 and 1912, when many of them listed their home as Coyr Zabet (Kfar Zabad), which was then controlled by Turkey. It included eighteen-year-old Amin Najm Nabhan, who in 1909 listed his previous residences as both Beirut and Syria. At that time, the Bekaa Valley was a Turk-controlled region of Syria, hence the confusion among American-born Nabhans when their grandparents called themselves Syrian, even though most remaining relatives live in what is now known as Lebanon.

The Bekaa Valley is at the southern cusp of the Fertile Crescent—one of the first cradles of agriculture in the Old World. But it has also been ancestral grounds for a number of my fellow Lebanese American writers and activists, from Ralph and Laura Nader to Vance Bourjailly and Greg Orfalea. We all grew up hearing stories of the Old Country, and, in most cases, the anciently inhabited landscape that our grandparents, aunts, and uncles referred to is none other than the Bekaa. In spring, it is a splendor of wildflowers; in fall, it is burgeoning with fruits of all shapes and sizes. And they are not merely fruits from nursery-raised trees or hybrid seed packets, but *baladi* varieties, ones that have been passed from hand to hand, sower to sower, for centuries.

For those of us with the surname Nabhan, the Old Country might just as well mean Yemen, Oman, Syria, Lebanon, Iraq, Iran, Tajikistan, or the Lamu Archipelago of Kenya. Today, the New Homeland can also mean Detroit, Boston, Brooklyn, the southwestern borderlands of the United States and Mexico, the coast of Veracruz and Yucatán in southern Mexico, Montreal, or São Paolo. The stories that tell of the movements between various ancestral grounds have largely faded from memory—until recently, that is—and the tribe's fundamental reasons for moving on continue to be obscured by time or reinterpreted by historians.

Our tribe has migrated, but so has the desert itself, as one place after another has been colonized, ravaged, and abandoned. Although the past itself does not stand still, it carries with it images that remind us of our links with our ancestors—the fragrances of rose water and frankincense, the tastes of wild thyme and sun-ripened dates, the smooth texture of walking sticks carved from the wood of a wild olive, the sound of the oud being plucked or the muezzin's call to prayer. The images themselves continue to echo through us. Our responses to them shift through time and may make much of this history sound quaint, absurd, distant, or irrelevant to the next generations of Banu Nabhani descendants to come along. They will have to tell their own versions of our tribal history in order to restore their own sense of place and kinship.

The ancestral lands themselves will outlast our memories of them and, after the scars have healed, will come upon their own natural ways of recovery, restore much of what they have lost over the centuries, and generate new seedlings of olives trees, frankincense shrubs, and wild herbs. A future generation will record in these landscapes something that we cannot even imagine seeing there today. The lands of our ancestors and the stories that are embedded in them will live on.

CHAPTER 7

Watching for Sign,
Tasting the Mountain Thyme

"LOOK WHERE YOU'RE WALKING, COUSIN!" my guide and distant kin Shibley Nabhan called to me from upslope. "You're walking through *sign!*"

I glanced down at my feet, which were for the first time planted on a ridge in the Anti-Lebanon Mountains, the geographic boundary between contemporary Lebanon and Syria. One foot was sinking into a bit of mud, the other more firmly resting on a limestone ledge above our ancestral village.

"Sign," I said to myself. *Sign?* No scat. No tracks. No browsed thyme, thistles, mallows, or mouse tips indicating that wild or domestic animals had passed this way.

"Sign, cousin? What sign?" I asked Shibley, who unlike me had walked this slope ten thousand times since childhood. Shibley Nabhan, who—unlike most of my cousins—had stayed close to his birthplace and still lived in Kfar Zabad, the "village of gifts." Some say the village is named in honor of an ancient Semitic god of giving. Herbalist, hunter, water-witcher, and mineral diviner: *that* Shibley, among my many relatives who share his first name. The Shibley who had ambled these slopes with shotgun, hoe, and olive-branch witching stick in tow. Employing himself as a contract archaeologist, occasional draftsman, freelance home builder, and teacher, Shibley had no fancy credentials other than an architect's license, but what he had instead was a great deal of "street smarts" about what this particular place could say to someone.

He hustled downslope to make sure I was getting the message.

"What sign?" I asked again, in case the arid breeze had blown my earlier question away from his ears. This time he was there by my side, leaning his elbow on my shoulder, twisting his salt-and-pepper mustache.

We both faced the same direction, looking down at the ground, intent on finding something that I had yet even to imagine.

"What *kind* of sign?" he said, pointing downslope with his foot. "This right here is a sign . . . maybe for treasure. But where they put it, I don't know. The people do it sometimes, these cut marks in the rock; other times, my God does it. *This one*? Not by God, maybe someone out here."

As he spoke, I began to see. A serpentine shape cut into the limestone. A snake's snout facing downhill.

"It's pointing to the place . . ." and as he shaped vision into words, he scrambled downslope and then up onto a slight rise, smack-dab in the midst of our great-grandparents' field.

"See, cousin?" he said, panting, as I caught up with him and caught my breath as well. "See? Big foot of the camel, that's what the snake was reaching for. There, you see?"

I saw: deep in a limestone outcrop, the impression of camel tracks. As vivid as my own shoeprint left in the mud some dozen yards upslope. These signs were not hand carved yesterday; they were perhaps from our nomadic clan's yesteryear.

"They might tell the secret of what is buried for us," Shibley smiled, hopeful.

"Buried beneath this limestone? Isn't this outcrop rather thick?" I asked, as if his hope were based on an incredulous assumption.

"No, not right here on the bedrock," Shibley said, pointing. "Where the camels are walking, you know. Somewhere right before us, here in the earth."

Earth. By that I guessed he meant the shallow lens of limy soil that had somehow remained upon this slope despite ten thousand years of grazing, farming, and foraging. I looked out into the Bekaa Valley far below us; still rich with topsoil, it formed the curve of the Fertile Crescent, where, some archaeologists claim, agriculture began. But here in the Anti-Lebanon Mountains, soil a foot and a half deep was a treasure in and of itself.

"Treasure . . . " Shibley murmured.

"Treasure buried under so little soil?" I asked, half in doubt, half in wonder. I hoped that he would read in my voice only the latter.

"Well, maybe not gold or old-time bronze. Maybe ancestral-ground boundary marker. Maybe where some miracle happened long time ago, marked by our forefathers, those who took camel as their sign. I can never tell what it is, first time. I come back here, over and over and over, trying to know: Which signs from my God, which from man?"

As we continued our descent toward the village, I could not take my eyes off the patches of exposed bedrock beneath my feet. Impressions of the hooves of goats and sheep. Human footprints. A bear claw, which Shibley had to point out to me, though it stood just in front of where the toes of my shoes touched the ground.

"We still have bears up above our highest pasture, sleeping in caves right now. They don't come down into pastures much, except when it's too dry. Then they get thirsty, they get hungry."

We heard bells above us. I kept looking down at the bear claw in the bedrock until Shibley nudged me. He turned to gaze upslope, high into the mountains. He touched my shoulder. I pivoted and realized that he was looking for the origin of the sound.

"It's the Badawī, whom you call Bedouin," he sighs. "Returning from our highest pasture with a few sheep and goats. We let them graze up here all summer, and they give us milk for making yogurt and cheese. The *lubni*, the yogurt, you know, it tastes different each week of the summer. That's because the sheep eat different medicines, the wild herbs. If they eat *zaatar*, the lubni tastes like zaatar."

ZAATAR. The wild mountain thyme of the Mediterranean. I had recently learned that it is a witches' brew of aromatic oils. Some chemicals in the thyme arsenal are so potent that they deflect or destroy insect pests. Others are pungent enough to deter browsing by larger animals, who, after a while, must move on to the next bush. And other aromatic oils exuded onto the leaf surfaces of thyme slow the loss of water from the plant as a whole, a worthy adaptation for an herb of arid climes.

The most peculiar characteristic of thyme, ecologist Yan Linhart discovered, is that different plants in the same mountain patch have different mixes of these aromatic oils. Some are better at repelling insects, others at deterring browsers, and still others at surviving drought. Collectively, a patch or population of mountain thyme can endure a panoply of stresses thanks to the heterogeneity of its membership. Each patch has its own peculiar flavor profile, so that no other zaatar will do for those who have grown up with one particular taste memory lodged in their mouths and minds.

As with the camel print held in the rock, you can read a patch of thyme in different ways if you open yourself to its presence. A treasure, a boundary marker, a little miracle.

During the same winter that I visited my grandfather's village for the first time, I also spent some time where other desert dwellers—ones who regularly harvest a wild oregano—live a seminomadic existence halfway around the world from Lebanon. I had been invited by my Seri Indian friends Adolfo Burgos and his wife, Amalia Astorga, to go with them to the now-abandoned village of Tecomate Well on Tiburón Island in the Sea of Cortés. They had not visited or harvested oregano there for some time, in part because the Mexican government had tried to sedentarize the Seri on the mainland, away from their island home. We took a *panga* boat ride out to the island to experience whether the oregano that grew there tasted different from the oregano that grew on the mainland. But soon we were distracted by another matter.

As soon as we arrived, Adolfo began to pray and sing while Amalia danced around the well, evoking the spirits of those who had been born, lived, and died there in the past. After two hours of pointing out details of their island heritage, describing each with great emotion, they felt drained and tired; we headed back toward the beach. But as we did, I noticed a giant sprawling cactus on the edge of the camp with sticks stuck into the ends of its arms. I suddenly realized that this multiarmed cactus, known in Spanish as *pitaya agria*, could not be found at all in the surrounding vegetation. It was, in fact, altogether rare on the north side of the island.

I had heard that plunging miniature harpoons into the tops of giant cacti was boys' play in Seri villages, but I had also heard that it was part of a sacred rite. Although I knew that Amalia was exhausted, I took her hand and walked over to the cactus with her, hoping that she might have enough on reserve at least to comment on the wood rods stuck high in the arms of this rare cactus. When we arrived at the base of the cactus, she looked up at it for a moment, saying nothing. Then she looked all around us and back toward the well, as if to gauge where it was placed.

"See," she said, pointing to one of the hand-carved rods stuck horizontally into an upper branch of spiny cactus, "this was inserted when a baby was born here. Since then, the cactus has grown upward from the height of the rod," and she pointed to the length of stem rising above where the stick had pierced the flesh of the cactus when it was younger. Then she added matter-of-factly, "Many of us have a plant like this, which our parents used to mark our birthplace, the very day we were born."

I did not fathom what she was saying. "The rod was put into the cactus when that spot was at the tip of the branch?"

She looked at me kindly, realizing that I couldn't understand it all. "The very day a child was born here, this cactus was transplanted to the very place where the child's placenta was buried."

"You mean the cactus was planted here and the rod was stuck into it the same day?" My mind reeled.

"Yes, so that later on they could show the child where he was born and how much the cactus had grown since then. Many of us know where our plants still grow. I know my saguaro cactus; it's over at Campo Onah. When I was a newborn, they hammered a stick into a cactus that they brought there from a place nearby. The plant belongs to me, the person born the same day. That's where they buried my placenta."

The Seri have a phrase to describe the place and time of birth, of burying your placenta back into the earth: *Hant Haxp M-ihiip. Hant*, they say, means "time, place, world, earth," and *Haxp M-ihiip* means "birth." A cactus to commemorate when and where you hit the ground, coming out of your mother, when and where your placenta went back into the earth. It is like the sign on the ground that my cousin Shibley is always seeking.

I can no longer imagine Seri territory without envisioning thousands of cacti and elephant trees transplanted across the desert, marking spots where babies first broke into light, where their grandparents and god-parents hammered or harpooned small sticks into plant flesh so that they could later show the children how much they had grown. I cannot imagine my grandparents' own natal grounds without remembering the ancient camel, sheep, and snake prints that will always surround them. Whatever I viscerally felt as my sense of place before this past winter, it has been indelibly changed by touching a transplanted cactus, deepened by walking among bedrock carvings of animal tracks, and flavored by mountain thyme that overwhelms the other wild fragrances in sheep milk. If I had not learned from my grandparents, uncles, aunts, and cousins how to look at, walk across, and taste the world, I would not have an inkling how to do that among other cultures, and my own meager life would be far poorer. But, as it stands, I have the scent of thyme on my hands, and cactus thorns have been tattooed into my memory.

Ever since I worked as a student intern at the first Earth Day headquarters in 1970, I have wondered why the so-called environmental movement is so clumsy at reaching out to speak to folks like my Lebanese cousin Shibley or my Seri Indian friends like Adolfo and Amalia. Or, more to the point, why it can hardly hear their voices or see their signs. Shibley's family has been involved in protecting a local wetland for migratory birds; Adolfo and Amalia have guided many trips to help protect both islands and coastal lagoons. And yet none of them is recognized much by large conservation organizations for the value of their traditional ecological knowledge. Conference after conference regarding the stewardship of nature, meeting after meeting of environmental activists, we receive group photos that largely look as though they are underexposed, as if they consist of monotones, not the range of colors, characters, and communities that collectively inhabit the earth. When I worked that spring of 1970 in Earth Day headquarters, I often slept on the mailbags in the headquarters office, a floor above a coffee shop where African, Caribbean, and Latin Americans would congregate late at night after the jazz and blues clubs had closed up their bars. Why did it seem, at the time, that those two floors of the same building represented divided worlds? Why were there so few people of color, people of the soil, among the environmentalists' ranks?

That gap has shrunk some since 1970, but few folks I know are content that it has shrunk enough. More than anything else I want to imagine a dialogue between cultures living on the same home ground; I want to hear a bunch of nature writers of different backgrounds swapping tales the way musicians in a jazz band swap riffs. I want us to find a groove where sounds from all around us, a wide range of natures, a wide range of cultures, play off one another, rising and diving, blending, diverging, skipping across the surface like perfectly thrown stones across a pond. I want to watch the ripples they make spread out and take on new shapes in every little cove where they flow. I want to see us as we begin to read one another's sign, as we taste the spiciness of one another's cuisines, as we hear the ancient ringing in the mountain echoing down to where we stand together, grateful to be in one another's presence.

III. Conflict and Convivencia

CHAPTER 8

Hummingbirds and Human Aggression

A View from High Tanks

I

IT WAS NOT EXACTLY what I'd call a desert resort, nor did I initially go there for sport. Instead, I pulled into a pit stop on the Devil's Highway— Camino del Diablo—in February 1991, for a reckoning of sorts. I had come to see if anything still grew in the tank tracks scarring the desert floor, to watch creatures battling for riches in patches along dry washes, and, last but not least, to reflect on human aggression. In particular, I was concerned by the growing perception among Americans that "Arabs are inherently aggressive and prone to fighting" and by a parallel perception among Arabs of the Middle East that "Americans claim they are peace loving, but carry the biggest sticks in the world."

Having more than once used the tagline "Arab American" as a cheap surrogate to describe the complexity of my own genetic and cultural identity, I belatedly realized that it was a sound bite that made neither my Arab kin nor my American neighbors too comfortable. As the first of many skirmishes among Arabs and Americans began in the Middle East in 1991, my own comfort level plummeted as well. It was time to go out in the desert, cool off, and reflect on human society at a safe distance from its congealed metropolitan masses.

The site of refuge I selected in Arizona's Stinking Hot Desert was more than twenty-five miles away from the nearest permanent human habitation, but less than four from a stretch of international border. That stretch, among the hottest on earth, had pulled me into its camps in six winters of the past sixteen. It is the heart of the Gran Desierto, the sunshot site of the many morality plays that desert rat writer Bill Broyles has so vividly penned. This year differed in a subtle manner; the atmosphere carried a palpable tension that I had failed to observe previously. I sensed that this weight in the air was somehow wafting in from a war far away, in

Iraq and Kuwait. I could not be sure, however, whether I was the one bringing that tension along with me or it was endemic to this land of little rain and yet hidden from my view in the past.

The origins of that tension had recently become my consuming passion. Like a lab scientist peering through a microscope to identify some debilitating disease, I became fixed on a global issue by concentrating my attention on this desert microcosm. I hoped to discover a morality that was not an abstraction, but something that emerged out of the local ecology and that I could adhere to in this place. This morality, I reckoned, must address a fundamental issue: "Are human societies fatally stuck in a genetic script of aggression against one another, whether or not such behavior is now adaptive?"

With every step I took around my desert camp, I sought clues. I found myself kicking up bones, grave markers, ammunition shells, historic warheads, and missile debris. At night, I glimpsed vapor trails emanating from various nomadic tribes, which occasionally came into my camp for a little water. The cliffs echoed with the calls of owls, their hooting souls reminding me of the presence of others among us.

So that you can understand the dynamics of this desert camp over the ages, perhaps I should echolocate its position in the world for you. It's below an ancient watering spot along the Camino del Diablo, where more than five hundred deaths have been recorded during the past century and a half. Some of these wayfarers died of thirst, some from broken dreams, some from ambush, and some in flight. Over millennia, various tribes have converged here as their migration routes intersected. They bartered, haggled, and battled over scarce resources, and they continually shifted the boundary lines of their territories. In recent decades, illegal immigrants from Latin America have attempted to cross some thirty miles of lava and sand in their desperate quest for work north of the border, and many have found death instead of jobs waiting for them. My camp below High Tanks is loaded with the dispirited bodies of these past encounters, for the historic cemetery and much of the prehistoric archaeology once evident here have been bulldozed and tank trampled by more recent military maneuvers.

I should explain, by the way, that I speak of two sorts of tanks. The latter are the armed and armored all-terrain vehicles of the U.S. Marines. The former, the High Tanks, are usually called Tinajas Altas because they were named in Spanish prior to the battle of the Alamo, when they were still part of Mexico. The High Tanks form a series of nine plunge pools, waterholes no bigger than bathtubs, naturally carved into the bedrock of a shady drainage that cascades five hundred feet down an abrupt granitic ridge.

Such cascades are seldom covered by waterfalls here in southwestern Arizona, where precipitation is so variable from year to year that all averages and ranges quickly lose their currency. Rain may fail twenty-six months at a time, but bombs will fall out of the sky quite frequently because the tanks lie in a bombing range jointly administered by the Marine Corps Air Station in Yuma and a Bureau of Land Management office in more distant Phoenix. The area is often closed to "public access" during periods of bombing exercises, tank maneuvers, and mock battles. It was here, in the late 1970s, that the U.S. military reputedly prepared for the ill-fated helicopter raid into Iran's arid turf to free American hostages; in 1991, it was used to prep for Operation Desert Storm. (Later, I would learn, it served as training ground for the Shock and Awe siege of Baghdad in 2003.)

I pondered the current operation and my own genetic history as an Arab American. A week before missiles were exchanged across the Saudi Arabia–Kuwait border, a Middle Eastern geographer sent me a few pages from Sir Arnold Talbot Wilson's 1928 history *The Persian Gulf*. I was simultaneously intrigued and appalled to read how history has repeated itself: eleven centuries ago a state of anarchy prevailed over the stretch of the Arabian Peninsula centered around present-day Oman, and my own family ultimately played a role in its outcome.

Taking advantage of the general chaos that occurred when the Abassid Empire fell apart, one Muhammad bin Nur wrested control of the region. Wilson noted that "[h]e cut off the hands and ears, and scooped out the eyes of the nobles, inflicted unheard-of outrages upon the inhabitants, destroyed the water-courses, burnt the books, and utterly destroyed the country."

Fortunately, as I remembered from earlier readings, Muhammad bin Nur's tyranny was met with "the wrath of an infuriated people," who disposed of his deputies but then went through seven imams of their own in less than thirty years. The area continued to be fraught with "intestine quarrels," Wilson tells us; then, "about the middle of the twelfth century, the Nabhan tribe acquired the ascendancy and ruled over the greater part of the interior of the country until the reestablishment of the Imamate in A.D. 1429; this tribe, however, continued to exercise considerable influence for quite two centuries longer . . . until . . . finally suppressed."

"Finally suppressed?" I wondered. "What had they done?" A little more historical sleuthing helped me find a frank acknowledgment of problems under Banu Nabhani rule by an eminent Arab historian, Humayd bin Muhammad bin Ruzayq, who lived during their reign: "[In short] . . . none of the Nabhani rulers was a just ruler, [and] most of them were known for their injustice and infidelity."

Stunned, I learned that my own Nabhan kinsmen had lost control of the spice routes edging the Arabian coast of the Persian Gulf due to their own internecine bickering. The civil war that destroyed the collective rule of the Banu Nabhani allowed the Portuguese to come in and take control of all the spice trade between Arabia and India. In the written histories of Oman, the long chronicle of Banu Nabhani bloodletting, infighting, and terrorizing appears to have dwarfed their material, social, and material accomplishments. My paternal ancestors had no doubt been as absorbed in the warring, the warding of territory, and the hoarding of resources as Muhammad bin Nur had been before them.

The very reading of these historic texts made me frown and emit a fatalistic groan. Did genes for pugnacity lie latent within me? Was I inevitably destined to war with my brothers, to wreak havoc on the world? And how much of the same bellicosity can be found not merely in my own bloodline, but in the genetic history of Everyman?

As foolish as it first seemed, I began to ask these questions of the desert around me, not rhetorically but literally: the desert that is an open book waiting to be read; the desert that, like Lyndon Johnson, so casually pulls up its shirt to show us its scars. And I ask these questions of the Sonoran Desert in particular—but because the Sonoran is hitched to every other desert in some essential way, the answer I hear has bearing on the Persian Gulf.

II

The sound of dive-bombing jars me from my slumber. Some hummingbirds call this place home, others migrate through it, but they all fight tenaciously for its resources. I hear metallic shrieks and *zings*—the latter not unlike the sound of glancing bullets—as the birds dive and chase one another. I roll over and cover my ears, but the high-pitched chittering has penetrated the tent walls. I must get up, go out, and face the music.

The morning sun has not yet come over the Cabeza Prieta range across the valley, but the fighting began well before daylight. I am camped in a wash that is a haven for hummingbirds, but to arrive here they have to cross a veritable hell, virtually devoid of the nectar and insect foods that their hyperactive metabolisms require. For miles in any direction, the surrounding desert flats and rocky slopes have little to offer the migrants of late winter. However, along a couple hundred yards of superficially dry watercourse leading down from the *tinajas* into the desert valley, the shrubbery is unusually dense. The native bushes form nearly impenetrable hedges of foliage along the banks of the wash, and some of these verdant walls look, at first glance, to be splattered with blood. The color, in fact, is supplied by thousands of crimson, floral tubes of *chuparosa* for which the shining warriors battle.

Chuparosa simply means "rose sucker" or "hummingbird" in Spanish. I am speaking of flowers so custom fit for pollination by hummingbirds that they bear the bird's name wherever they grow. The chuparosa flower is elongate for hummingbird bills and tongues, a chalice filled to the brim with nectar each dawn. The bushes bloom through late winter in frost-free zones, tiding the birds over until the coming of spring stimulates other plants to blossom. Their bright color attracts hummingbirds from some distance away. In turn, the winged creatures transport the "sperm of floral sex" from one bush to the next, ensuring cross-pollination. The birds' iridescent heads become discolored by the thousands of pollen grains plastered onto them as they probe the flowers, hovering at their entranceways. I saw this same phenomenon once while at a desert oasis in the Middle East, where a Palestinian sunbird dipped its head into the blossom of a pomegranate tree and came out glowing like the sun.

As I marvel over the perfect fit between hummer and blossom, another hummer comes along—and a high-speed chase begins. The Rufous Hummingbird and Costa's Hummingbird dogfight over the flower that is seemingly suited to fit both their needs, while I wonder how their belligerence is viewed by the Bambi Bunch, those who see all animals as cute, cuddly, and constantly in balance and at peace. In the blazing sun of a Tinajas Altas morning, I take a hard look at the desert, its creatures and flowers, trying to keep my own rose-colored glasses from tainting the picture as nature films and glossy magazine features so often do. I concede that Nature behaves unlike model members of either the Tooth-and-Claw Hunting Club or the Benevolent Sorority of Nurturing Networkers. Nature, to my knowledge, has not recognized that adherence to any anthropomorphic construct is a requisite for existence. I try to put such filters aside, wanting to read the desert's own pattern without superimposing others upon it.

So I walk up and down the wash looking for hummingbirds, soon catching a flurry of avian activity in a dense patch of chuparosa bushes. I sit upslope between two battlefields and not far away from a third. At one, a male Costa's is perching on a mesquite branch overlooking a mound of flowers. He darts out to hover in front of a blossom or two and sucks up their nectar. Then he suddenly turns to chase away another small bird. I watch as he whips away after a brother Costa's or possibly a Black-chinned. Minutes later he chases an Anna's that ventures too close to his treasure. Although Costa's adults are somewhat smaller than these other species, they are roughriders, well adapted to such desert conditions. It is not surprising that they are the most abundant warriors in this wash.

I guess they must already be nesting and mating here. Down the wash a little way, I spot the purple throat (characteristic of Costa's) doing a bizarre dance; he is flying a huge U-shape, an arc perhaps sixty to eighty feet from tip to tip. He hovers at the end of the arc, high up, then swoops down to the ground with a high-pitched buzz; soon he begins again, tracing the same arching pathway. From my vantage point, I can't see a female at the base of his courtship loop, but suspect that this aerial ballet is not being done to flatter *me*.

In the next patch over, I have trouble telling who has been holding the territory most of the time. Whenever I can identify the actors in a Painted Desert drama, a Rufous male has the upper hand over a Costa's.

Rufous Hummingbirds do not nest here; they migrate up through California when the ocotillo blooming begins, and some continue as far as Alaska. The wandlike ocotillos are spread widely over the rocky ridges and flats of the Sonoran and Mojave deserts. Their populations burst from bud sequentially—south to north—giving migrants a drawbridge extending northward. When cold winter weather has postponed ocotillo flowering several weeks, the hummers sometimes try to migrate anyway—in advance of peak flowering. In such years, ocotillo fruit are left with low seed set when their pollinators miss their date.

The ocotillo-flowering fest is an event that will begin here in another week or so. In most years, I recall, migrants such as the Rufous arrive in late February just prior to the opening. They pack into the chuparosa patches already occupied by Costa's and Anna's, adding to the territorial tension. The late William Calder—a dear friend of mine, an avian phys-iologist, and a Quaker pacifist who discovered a remarkable lifelong fidelity of hummingbirds to their nesting sites—also observed Rufous individuals allegiant to particular stops along their normal migration route. Even though the Rufous do not nest at Tinajas Altas as do Costa's and Anna's, their stake in this place is more than a one-shot deal. Unlike certain birds that become territorial only around courtship, breeding, and nesting, Rufous Hummingbirds lay claim even to sets of resources en route to their breeding ground and fight tenaciously to keep other hum-mers out in the cold.

This fact strikes me as curious, for I had supposed that birds become territorial only when needing to exclude other males of their own species from access to potential mates or to guard enough food to raise a brood. Melees between migrants don't make sense at first. I weave my way down the wash, wondering about this seeming incongruity. I then recall that a mentor of mine when I first studied ecology—avian ecologist David Lyon—probed this very problem three hundred miles to the east of Tinajas Altas, in the Chiricahuas.

When I contact Lyon later on, he responds to my questions on hum-mingbird behavior with the fine specificity that characterizes the best of ecologists: "Where were you?" he asks. "There are great differences in territoriality in the winter depending on the area. But all of these little rascals are opportunistic and will set up territories any time of the year if rewards are sufficient."

If rewards are sufficient. Lyon views the driving force of hummingbird territoriality as the defense of dense caches of food during times of the year when there are few alternative energy resources. Because humming-birds must consume close to half their weight in sugar each day to main-tain normal activities, finding a concentrated source of food for their fifty to sixty meals per day is a palpable problem. Territories at the Tinajas, then, should be most pronounced when chuparosa nectar production is sufficiently high to make the exclusion of other birds worth the price of the energy expended in defense. Imagine a chuparosa patch as an oil field thick with wells, in a country with few other energy resources developed. That's where the troops will hover.

I have a chance to explore Lyon's notion a month later when I return to my camp, not long after the peak of ocotillo flowering on the surrounding flats. The wash so aggressively and noisily guarded in early March is in April as quiet as a reading room. There are still hummers around, but no frenzy of flowering attracts them as before. Most of the resident birds have dispersed after nesting to draw upon the widely scattered ocotillo blossoms that remain. The migrants have moved on, so the number of competitors for any single patch of flowers is low. Territorial shows, for the most part, are canceled.

Lyon himself had tied the story down another way. He verified that territoriality among different species of hummers is truly adaptive and not simply a misdirected means of venting innate aggression on other species that a male has mistakenly identified as competing for his potential partners. For his test, Lyon enticed a Blue-throated Hummingbird to establish a territory in an area circumscribed by ten sugar-filled feeders, two placed in the center of the area and eight in a circle on the periphery. Over the following period, he held constant the amount available to the bird, but once a day he moved the eight feeders on the periphery farther out from the midpoint, enlarging the area over which the sugar sources were distributed.

Lyon was not surprised when the Blue-throated male took to chasing other hummers out of the artificial territory, regardless of the area it covered. In fact, this male at first spent twice as much time in dogfights around the hummingbird feeders as males typically spend defending natural patches of flowers. The trouble came as the feeders were spread over a larger area. The Blue-throated initially attempted to defend the expanded arena, but the number of competitors entering it increased to two-and-a-half times what it was in the original small territory. In the smaller arena, the territorial male chased after the majority of all hummers trespassing into his turf, irrespective of their species identity. When the sugar was set out over the largest area, he was forced to become more selective in his combat; he needed more time to pursue competitors across the longer distances between feeders and more time flying to reach the various feeders to refuel himself. The Blue-throated male therefore shifted his strategy. Rather than wearing himself out with incessant jousting, he opted for adaptability. He had tolerated the presence of females of his kind all along, but now he also permitted Black-chinned Hummingbirds to forage on the periphery. Although the Black-chins outnumbered the other hummers at this time, they were small and therefore most easily expelled when resources became scarce. Magnificents were tolerated in the oversized territory as well.

At last, defense against all comers became tenuous. Lyon's Blue-throated male allowed a few competing males of its kind to feed without being ejected. Still, whenever he chased other Blue-throated males, he pursued them for greater distances than he flew to repel other species. If another bird was seen as a competitor for *both* food and sex, the aggressive tendency of territorial males toward him remained in place.

Place per se is not what the birds are defending. They are after a finite amount of nectar, pollen, and bugs required to stay alive and to pass on their genes. If they can glean those foods without much territorial warfare or pyrotechnics, they will do so, whether from a small area or from a large one.

Their lives cost something, as do ours. On a late winter day, an Anna's Hummingbird must spend one minute out of every nine feeding in order to fuel its metabolism. Its hovering and flying demand ten times the calories per ounce of flesh that people need when running at full clip. If you give a hummer a feeder full of "junk food," it will reduce its foraging effort to a tenth of what it would otherwise. Nonetheless, a male does not fill up all this newly found "leisure time" with warfare. Even when you give him a territory literally dripping with sticky-sweet sucrose water, his foraging efficiency increases tenfold, but his time pestering intruders only doubles.

If we put this behavior in terms of an ecological maxim, we would say that a male hummer will defend a patch of riches only to the extent that it is truly "adaptive" to do so. When battling becomes too costly relative to the food security it brings, he will relax what many observers have assumed to be unrelenting, genetically determined hostility. Here is where the genetic determinists (and fatalists) have led us astray: they claim that it is our "animal nature" to be aggressive, yet even animals stereotyped as interminably warlike *can* suspend their territorial behavior. They opt for peace whenever their essential needs are met or when the cost of territorial behavior becomes too high.

When I ask my colleague Amadeo Rea about his take on such phenomena after studying birds for forty years, he points out to me the simplest of facts: "Hummingbird fighting—or warfare, if you wish to call it that—is not really homologous to human activities of the same name. How many dead hummers do you find in the chuparosa patch? How many bloodied, maimed victims? Their fighting . . . is probably only to exclude, not to destroy, a rival male."

The Aztecs called the hummingbird *huitzitzil*, "shining one with (a weaponlike) cactus spine." Yet for all its feistiness, the hummingbird does not embody the incessant irascibility attributed to it by certain historic and modern observers. Do such ascriptions actually tell us more about the Aztecs or the sociobiologists than they do about the bird itself? If human warfare is not homologous to that found in other animal species, what is its derivation? Is it somehow peculiar to the genes of *Homo sapiens*, or do we speak falsely when we claim fatalistically that human aggression is genetically determined? I go back into the desert to answer these questions, a colorblind botanist seeking clues that those with normal vision may not be able to detect. And I turn my vision from the hummingbirds—most of which have taken flight by this time—to the human being, whose tracks are still evident all around me.

III

Now it is April. I'm up above the desert floor on the ridge overlooking the High Tanks. Last night I tucked my sleeping bag into a rock shelter, a cave of sorts shared with an old friend and a few packrats. We had hoped to see desert bighorn come in for water. This niche in the granite formerly kept O'odham hunters out of sight until they were ready to jump the wild rams and ewes trapped in the canyon. I dream of seeing sheep approach, and I imagine myself a primitive hunter from centuries past, hot in the pursuit of big game.

Suddenly I am jogged from my reverie by the realization that we are being pursued. My friend Susan Zwinger has noticed that an armored vehicle has lumbered up out of a wash, heading straight toward our parked pickup truck on the desert floor below us.

We watch, silent, hidden in the rocks, as the tanklike all-terrain vehicle stops fifty yards away from our truck. Its passengers do not immediately get out to breathe the fresh morning air. We wait for the doors to open. More than a minute passes.

All doors swing open simultaneously, and six soldiers land on the ground, automatic rifles in hand, spreading out. They slowly stalk the truck, fingers ready on the triggers. Forming a semicircle ten feet out from the back and sides of the truck, weapons aimed at all openings, the men look ready to move in for the kill.

"Campers!" I yell, immediately regretting it. In the folk taxonomy of the military, the word *campers* does not necessarily conjure up a contradistinction to *drug runners*, *wetbacks*, or *Arab terrorists*. It does not bring the same sigh of relief that *garter snake* brings when the choice might be *sidewinder*. Half the armed men now point their weapons toward the wash from which they sense my yell emerging. I wince, remembering another time on the Camino del Diablo when a border guard held me at gunpoint, my hands behind my back, belly to the ground, for a half-hour of questioning. He had been sure that I was a drug smuggler, unconvinced that anyone who arrived on his borderline beat at dawn was there merely to watch birds. From that distasteful experience, I knew that I had to assure the boys below that they were not stalking aliens from another continent.

"Campers! It's okay! It's okay!" I yell again, waving my Panama hat back and forth in case they needed a moving target. The echoes seem to confuse them, as they have confused me when I have tried to locate a calling owl while standing near its position below the cliffs. Then, one of the GIs spots my movement, raises field glasses to his eyes, and gives Susan and me a quick once-over. Another lowers his rifle and raises his binoculars as well. There is some talking, largely below earshot, all beyond comprehension. They all release their fingers from triggers and sulk back to the armored vehicle. Another minute passes, and they are gone.

The season of heightened hummingbird aggression has passed, but my preoccupation with human aggression is bursting its buds. The military visitors to Tinajas Altas have departed silently, without incident, but that does not leave me much solace. As Susan and I descend into camp and return to the truck, the air there is choked with a sense of aggression. It is perhaps like the feeling of violation that one feels for months after one's house has been robbed; physical violence may have been avoided, but any measure of psychological peace has been shattered.

At the same time, I feel foolish for expecting human presence in a place such as the High Tanks to have any smackings of tranquility. As my mind rolls over just a few of the incidents that have been staged here over the years, I realize that few desert routes in the world have been soaked in as much blood as has the Camino del Diablo. I remember how Teddy Roosevelt's son Kermit described Tinajas Altas and its desperados during a hunting trip in the August heat of 1910:

> This is a grim land, and death dogs the footsteps of those who cross it. Most of the dead men [buried below the Tanks] were Mexicans who had struggled across the desert only to find the tanks dry. Each lay where he fell, until, sooner of later, some other traveler found him and scooped out for him a shallow grave, and on it laid a pile of rocks in the shape of a rude cross. Forty-six unfortunates perished here at one time of thirst. They were making their way across the deserts to the United States, and were in the last stages of exhaustion when they reached these tanks. But a Mexican outlaw named Blanco reached the tanks ahead of them and bailed out the water, after carefully laying in a store for himself not far away. By this cache he waited until he felt sure that his victims were dead; he then returned to the tanks, gathered the possessions of the dead, and safely made his escape.

Add to the human corpses at least twice as many livestock carcasses, and you would arrive at a paradise-and-lunch for vultures were it not for the long wait between courses. When carrion feeders were not enticed to dine in such an out-of-the-way place, the flesh slowly sizzled to beef-jerky consistency on the skilletlike desert pavement. I've measured temperatures of 170 degrees at ground level near here, on a summer day that was not particularly hot. In 1861, when New York mining engineer Raphael Pumpelly rode the *camino* during the period of peak heat, he wondered if he had stepped beyond the familiar into another world. In his *Across America and Asia*, published in 1870, he writes:

> We were approaching the Tinajas Altas, the only spot where, for a distance of 120 miles, water might at times be found. It was a brilliant moonlit night. On our left rose a lofty sierra, its fantastic sculpturing weird even in the moonlight. Suddenly we saw strange forms indefinable in the distance. As we came nearer our horses became uneasy, and we saw before us animals standing on the side of, and facing the trail. It was a long avenue between rows of mummified cattle, horses and sheep.

Pumpelly's handwritten journal, not published until 1918, gives the incident in more detail:

The pack animals bolted and Poston and I rode through with difficulty. Ten or twelve years before, during the time when meat was worth in California almost its weight in gold dust, it paid to take the risk of losing on this desert nearly all of the herd, if a few survived. If no water was found at the Tinajas, most or all of the animals and some of the men would die. In the intensely dry and pure air there was no decomposition. All the dead simply became mummies. The weird avenue had been made by some travelers with a sense of humor and fertile imagination which had not been deadened by thirst.

A thirst of another sort drove miners and buckaroos across the desert and moved Blanco the Bandito to empty all the water out of the plunge pools: greed. Life did not matter as much as money or material possessions. Those who rode down the Camino del Diablo did not care about the places they were passing through or the life they might encounter along the way. Some of the native O'odham, first recorded in residence at Tinajas Altas in 1699, had adopted the same attitude by the mid–nineteenth century. They made a pastime out of robbing and infrequently killing forty-niners en route to California.

Such conduct disturbed their neighbor Tom Childs, the first white man to marry into the Sand People, or Hia c-eḍ O'odham. Tom finally asked one of the Indian bandits, José Augustín, "Why did you kill the camino travelers?" and Augustín responded with matter-of-fact brevity: "For the sugar, tobacco, and coffee."

This quip must have struck Childs as anomalous, for the O'odham— including the Sand People—have been known for a century and a half as "the Peaceful People." In anthropologist Ashley Montagu's global search for cultural models of nonaggressive behavior, the historic O'odham were included among the two dozen societies least prone to violence.

Despite recent rises in family violence where substance abuse has affected them, the O'odham people as a whole can still be characterized as having a pacific temperament. I have had the good fortune to work, eat, and sleep in the homes of several O'odham families over the past sixteen years, and I have been moved by their peaceable nature: a humility and a live-and-let-live commitment to conflict evasion underscore most of their cross-cultural interactions with neighbors and visitors. The historic litera-ture on the "Pima" or "Desert Papago" or "Sand Papago," as they were formerly called, reiterates that the O'odham avoided violence whenever possible.

During World War II, with the support of their elders, the young men of an entire village refused to be inducted into the military. Other O'odham, of course, have dutifully participated in the armed services rather than raise a ruckus, the best known being the Pima hero at Iwo Jima, Ira Hayes. Like Hayes, however, many came back from the service profoundly dis-turbed by what they had participated in, and some died from the alcohol or drugs they took to deal with the cultural collisions. Anthropologist Ruth Underhill argued that for the traditional O'odham, "War . . . was not an occasion for prestige as with the Plains tribes or of booty as with the Apache. It was a disagreeable necessity. The enemy . . . or anything that had touched him, was taboo. Therefore all booty was burned and the man who had killed an enemy or who had been wounded by him had to go through a long ordeal of purification."

These words are echoed by ethnohistorians Clifford B. Kroeber and Bernard L. Fontana, who worked together for three decades on the major work *Massacre on the Gila*, concerning intertribal warfare among South-west Indians: "While they were perfectly capable of taking the offensive, Pimas and Papagos [O'odham] seemed to have done so only when re-venge was called for or as a counter-offensive to protect lives and property. There is little to suggest that northern Pimans ever made raids for the sole purpose of obtaining booty. . . . Neither does it appear that northern Pimans engaged in ritualized formal battles with their Apache and Yava-pai enemies [after] 1698."

Indeed, the first O'odham raids on Camino del Diablo travelers may have been in response to finding a year's supply of water consumed by cattle, horses, and journeymen during a single day's stopover. When Padre Eusebio Kino came into the area around 1700, his livestock drank dry one tinaja after another. In response, the able-bodied O'odham men did not immediately fight, but fled instead, leaving only the smallest children and infirm elders to be baptized by the Jesuit father. It was not until Anglos and Mexicans began draining the plunge tanks of the camino with frequency— during the California gold rush—that the O'odham sought to discourage travelers along the route.

Like the !Kung Bushmen of the Kalahari and Australian Aborigines of the Red Centre, the O'odham of the Sonoran Desert developed traditions that put a damper on aggressive behavior and a premium on cooperation. In *Anger: The Misunderstood Emotion*, psychologist Carol Tavris writes of desert nomads so dependent on unpredictable environments that "[t]heir only insurance against hard times is each other. No individual can lay-in a supply of frozen pizzas and beer in the event of famine and drought, and no individual could long survive on his or her own. . . . Under such conditions, any antisocial or angry outbursts threaten the whole group; so it is to the [desert dweller's] interest to avoid direct physical confrontation or violence, and to be suspicious of individuals who cannot control their behavior or their tempers."

Further, Tavris sees nothing innately aggressive in human beings: "It is the world, not the genes, that determines which way it will go." Yet I've recently come to realize that this issue is a virtual battleground within academia. Sociobiologist E. O. Wilson asserts in his book *On Human Nature* that "human beings have a marked hereditary predisposition to aggressive behavior." He does concede, however, that aggression is not tied to a single gene, adaptive syndrome, or racial lineage, and he expresses other ambivalences, arguing that our territorial expressions often respond to the same resource-scarcity problems that direct other animals toward territoriality, but at the same time that our aggressive expressions are peculiar. "Most significantly of all," he asserts, "the human forms of aggressive behavior are species-specific: although basically primate in form, they contain features that distinguish them from aggression in all other species."

To my mind, Wilson shifts between two parallel ruts, arguing both that we have aggressive (animal) responses *and* that our scholars and political leaders can lead us into more diplomatic resolutions of conflict if they choose pacifism as a goal. He hardly takes into account the vast terrain between these ruts. His scientific parables are fixed on the notion that all behavior can be explained by understanding the evolutionary history we share with other species. Although rightly emphasizing that we respond to many social or environmental stresses and conflicts much the way other organisms do—there are only so many options—he often glosses over critical differences in context and intent.

Nevertheless, one of Wilson's paradigms may shed light on the hummingbirds that become territorial around dense patches of chupa-rosa in the middle of nowhere *and* on the O'odham, who do the same with plunge pools. A territory, Wilson notes, invariably

> contains a scarce resource, usually a steady food supply, shelter, space for sexual display, or site for laying eggs. . . . [T]erritorial behavior evolves in animal species only when the vital resource is *economically defensible*: the energy saved and the increase in survival and reproduction due to territorial defense outweigh the energy expended and the risk of injury and death. . . . [I]n the case of food territories the size of the defended area is at or just above the size required to yield enough food to keep the resident healthy and able to reproduce. Finally, territories contain an "invincible center." The resident animal defends the territory far more vigorously than intruders attempt to usurp it, and as a result the defender usually wins. In a special sense, it has the "moral advantage" over tres-passers. (emphasis in original)

I tend to agree with Wilson that it is somehow "natural" for indigenous desert people to defend a waterhole from intruders, much the same way hummingbirds' territorial pugnacity is natural. But because such ag-gressiveness is oftentimes relaxed when resources become more abun-dant or widely dispersed, neither the hummers nor the hunter-gatherers seem inexorably fixed on fighting. Be that as it may, cross-cultural com-parisons suggest that most societies fight for reasons other than those obviously related to their immediate physical survival. Only 10 percent of so-called primitive cultures maintain a constant peace with their neigh-bors. For the 64 percent that skirmish with neighbors at least once every two years, many but not all of their conflicts concern competition for basic resources. Cultural evolution has left us with tensions not easily explained by addressing only the driving forces of natural selection: the need for food, water, and shelter; the urge to reproduce and keep our genes "alive" in the form of offspring. This focus is why there is something profoundly disturbing—probably unprecedented in mammalian evolu-tion until ten thousand years ago—about Blanco the Bandit's actions. By draining the plunge pools, he left all later travelers without access to an essential resource. If there is something peculiar about us latter-day hu-man beings, it is our ability to opt for destroying a resource essential for everyone's survival rather than simply controlling a competitor's access to it. In this new game—untried in an evolutionary sense—neither resident nor intruder ultimately wins. As the resource vanishes, all potential users are inevitably vanquished.

IV

For weeks, the tension had mounted. Young, hormone-charged men stood on the south side of a line—like so many hummingbirds waiting for the ice to break up to the north, for the season to burst with activity. First Lieutenant John Deedrick likened the mood on the front lines to the waiting in a blind while hunting deer: "Just like being in a tree stand. You're cold and miserable and you just have to wait."

Then Desert Storm let loose like an ejaculatory release from an eighteen-year-old: after an all-out war of some one hundred hours, the boys were done. The troops were coming home, having freed the oil fields of Kuwait from a despot's control. American soldiers had regained the solid manly image deflated during the 1960s.

"By God," the first President Bush exclaimed, "we've kicked the Vietnam syndrome once and for all!"

Lingerie sales in America reached an all-time high as women swooned for the victors. The boys were a bit embarrassed, as an anonymous soldier back from Persian Gulf explained on a Scottsdale, Arizona, morning talk show: "I think its kinda shallow that a girl might want to make it with me just because I was over there. . . . Fun, but shallow."

As anthropologists Fontana and Kroeber see it, ever since farming overtook hunting as society's primary means of support, young men have been trying to figure out what they can excel at that women cannot. The hunter's prowess, tenacity, and dignity, which once won him access to the most attractive and fecund mates, evaporated when men and women began to share in the chores of agrarian society. Women had already been tending plants for centuries, domesticating them and possibly bringing in far more calories than male "breadwinners." As landscapes became tamed and men spent less time on the mythic wild proving grounds, they abdicated a primordial connection that had given them their meaning. What many people came to feel, Kroeber and Fontana have recently said aloud: "Women could do all the work necessary for society's physical survival. Males were potentially persons of great leisure. Or," as they rather bluntly state, "males were potentially all but useless."

Men swerved off course, from the sacramental and nutritionally justified bloodletting of hunting to that of warfare, even when gains did not justify the risks. Another hunger grew in men's loins that made them want to taste blood, to be on top. And this hunger, seldom satisfied, sticks with many men today. Never in history have men been so useless; a woman can now go to a sperm bank and be fertilized without ever having to touch her child's biological father. No wonder Robert Bly's poem "Gathering of Men" has captured center stage in a formerly floundering men's movement. It sees the male loss of meaning beginning with the Agricultural Revolution, which took men out of contact with the wild, disbanding the fraternity of the Big Woods.

No boot camp or campus fraternity hazing has ever made up for that lack. Military service, far from the mythic rite of passage that it once was for males in many societies, has become an objectified routine of monitoring computer printouts and calculating missile trajectories from remote locations. The bombing of targets has become so depersonalized by the jargon that one might as well be playing a video game. The young technicians simply "took out their targets" and euphemistically referred to any human losses in those debilitated places as "collateral damage."

American audiences responded to the Gulf War with much the same fervor they usually reserve for the made-for-TV Super Bowl. Arab bashing became a new spectator sport: "Operation Desert Storm" cards came with bubble gum in packages remarkably similar to those in which our boys find the faces of Larry Bird, Bo Jackson, and Michael Jordan.

Even if the government's pathological lies about the war disturbed some Americans, it was fortunate for Bush that Saddam Hussein still seemed downright evil, whereas we only seemed sick. Of course, that perception was largely influenced by the White House media machine. Who else could be better cast in the role of Blanco the Bandit than Saddam Hussein himself? Rather than emptying out the tinajas of all their water, he shrewdly set fire to the scarcest resource underpinning our global economy: fossil fuel. While more than five hundred wells burned like battle torches day after day, enough oil was going up in smoke to meet a tenth of the world's daily consumption.

"If hell had a National Park, this would be it," mourned the U.S. Environmental Protection Agency's director William Reilly on the *Today* show just after his return from Kuwait on May 7, 1991, hardly two months after the Gulf War "cease-fire." The fires, of course, had not ceased: it would take months to extinguish all of them, and for each month that the blazes continued unabated, they added to the atmosphere as much as 1.0 million tons of sulfur dioxide, 100,000 tons of nitrogen oxides, and 2.5 million tons of oil soot—the latter amount being more than four times the monthly emissions from the entire United States. According to desert ecologist Tony Burgess, who went to the Persian Gulf with Friends of the Earth to assess the environmental damage resulting from the war, this brief set of skirmishes and bombings of oil wells contributed 4 percent of the world's total carbon release by the end of 1991, thereby accelerating global warming over the long run.

And yet the first President Bush persistently claimed that Desert Storm made the victory swift and the long-term damages minimal. Unfortunately, his antiseptic war was never that at all; more than one hundred thousand people were dead within a month, and twice that many were wounded, crippled, and contaminated with toxins. Many more people were deprived of potable water and food for months on end, and it is now estimated that only one-tenth of the total number of deaths occurred during the "official" war. Environmental destruction proceeded on an unprecedented scale and left unsanitary remains that will persist indefinitely.

To console us, William Reilly announced in doublespeak (during the same *Today* interview) that "President Bush cares as much about the environment as he did about winning the war."

However, the condition of the fragile desert left behind by a million troops does not give credence to this platitude. Scars left by helter-skelter driving of military vehicles will be seen in the vegetation and soils for anywhere from one hundred to one thousand years. In some places, observers found the desert biologically sterile following the war; elsewhere, the remaining plants were covered with a crust of soot, oil, and wind-drifted sand. Massive defense berms interrupted watercourses, and countless bomb craters were not exclusively the result of Iraqi actions. The U.S. Air Force admits that it left behind nearly nine thousand tons of undetectable explosive materials in desert areas. Regarding exploded refineries and burning lakes of oil, the culpability is blurred. "Who knows who set what off?" asked Tony Burgess during a telephone interview. His succinct description of the place says it all: "The country was so trashed. It literally was a vision of hell."

We have only an inkling of how large that hellish landscape will eventually be, but Burgess assured me that the oil fires are bound to have profound, pervasive global ramifications. Using the greasy soot particles resulting from the burning oil fields as but one example, he told me that "effects from the Kuwaiti smoke plume [had] already been picked up in Australia and Hawaii," more than eight thousand miles away from their source. From the snows of the Himalayas to the headwaters of the Blue Nile, acid rain and carbon soot accumulated at unprecedented levels.

Petroleum engineer John Cox regards the magnitude of carbon soot from Kuwait, Iraq, and Saudi Arabia to be more concentrated and therefore more devastating than what would be expected were a nuclear winter to occur. He explained why the Kuwaiti smoke plume dispersed so widely: "If you are in a rainy area, a very high proportion of the smoke is going to be washed out. If, however, you are in an area that is already dry— and the microclimate around Kuwait is very dry—and you have intense temperature, then the chances are that the smoke cloud will go to a much greater height than the nuclear war simulations suggest. . . . [There will be] a major effect upon the growth of vegetation and crops."

This is not the maverick opinion of one self-styled expert, but that of the Greenpeace organization as well, which claims that the Gulf War ranks as one of the most ecologically destructive conflicts ever. According to environmental activist Andre Carothers, Kuwaiti officials concede that the environmental damages of the war are far more crippling than any material losses incurred during the hundred days of armed conflict. And that, to my mind, is the fatal divergence of our path from that of our sometimes pugnacious biological ancestors and neighbors on this planet. Although sociobiological scholars may still smugly argue that "we are far from being the most violent animal," the damage our kind has done is suffusive enough to be all-encompassing.

Hummingbirds skirmishing over chuparosa, O'odham and Quechan Indians vying for a waterhole, or Kuwaitis and Iraqis battling over an oil field may appear to be parallel parables of territorial disputes over scarce resources in the desert. But the latter type of battle has the capacity to damage a broad range of resources required for life now and in the future—

indeed, to damage irreparably the capacity for life support within our planet's atmosphere. Gone are the days when ritualized warfare affected control over only one waterhole, one food-gathering ground, one territory.

The verbal antagonism between Saddam Hussein and George Bush on television was a pathetic throwback to esoteric jousting by medieval sportsmen who lived in a time when the stakes were low and the damage local. We can no longer speak of competition for a single, concentrated resource; a life-support system dependent on widely dispersed, vitally important resources is now under threat. The number of wars within and between nations increased during the twentieth century, as compared to other centuries, despite pacifying efforts by the United Nations and other mediating bodies. If leaders such as Bush or Hussein had the mentality of a hummingbird, it would be clear to them that the resources crucial to our survival are no longer economically or ecologically defensible through territorial behavior. These resources are too diffuse, too globally interdependent, to be worth the risks such leaders take. But what a hummingbird can surmise with its sense in a matter of hours or days, our species must muddle through, argue about, and even shed blood over for decades.

V

I am back in the dead of summer on a desert wash near the international border where hummingbird bushes like the chuparosa exhibit a few last, ill-fated flowers withering in the heat. A fire has burned a patch along the border today. Dusty whirlwinds are everywhere, turning and churning in the drought-stricken air. A hummingbird whirrs by me. I turn to see if he is being chased, then back to see if he is in hot pursuit of another. He is not. We stop on opposite sides of the wash, which is wide enough to let us pause for a moment without feeling that we are on top of one another.

As I pause, I think of the O'odham name for Tinajas Altas: O'ovak, "Arrowhead Sunk." The Sand People tell about two of their fellow O'odham who climbed to one of the ridges overlooking the steep-sided canyon where the precious pools of water are found today. One of these two warriors challenged the other to a contest: Who could shoot an arrow all the way across the canyon to the far ridge?

As my O'odham friends tell the story, the first man's arrow cleared the canyon, but the other man's did not. Instead, it glanced against the bedrock in the drainage, skipped along, then sank into the granite. Wherever it had struck rock, however, a pool of water formed, and the O'odham and their neighbors have used these plunge pools ever since. Retelling this story, my friends express their gratitude for the unlikely appearance of water wherever it emerges in the desert.

I turn to the hummingbird and think, "Who, then, won the contest? The warrior demonstrating the greatest facility with weaponry or the one who helped make a lasting resource for all people?" Laughing at myself, at the long and winding trails my answers take, I leave the wash with one last gesture to the hummer. "You must be my teacher," I offer, palms open to his direction. "We're here together." I am beginning to learn what we share in common—this earth—and what differences in behavior I cannot bear to let come between us.

CHAPTER 9

Other Voices, Human and Avian
Reconnecting Place with Peace in a Broken World

I. A Stone, a Birdsong, a Prayer for the Displaced

A CHUNK OF PALE, limy dolomite sits on my desk, a fragment of my ancestors' homeland. I sometimes fit it inside my fist to remind me of the very ground from which my grandmother Julia was torn just before World War I. Once a chink between larger, more durable cobbles in the dry masonry walls that cradled my grandmother during her girlhood, this stone speaks to me like no other.

The day I plucked that chunk of dolomite from the wall of my *sitti's* cobblestone hut in Kfar Zabad I noticed how the hut itself echoed the texture and color of the ridges flanking the Bekaa Valley. Those ridges rise into the Anti-Lebanon Mountains, along the present-day border of Lebanon with Syria, a place less than 150 miles from bullet-riddled Jerusalem and less than 200 miles from bombed-out Iraq. This little farming village —from which some of my ancestors fled a century ago—also recently came under missile fire for the first time in years.

Like the stone that now rests on my desk, my grandmother was displaced from her place of origin in Kfar Zabad; in her case, just as the first decade of the twentieth century came to a close. During the following decade, my grandparents were forced to flee from Lebanon to Syria and then out of a Turkish port to America. Warring was almost constant, and the Turks conscripted more than 240,000 Arabs into their forces. Roughly 40,000 of those conscripted were killed, and another 150,000 deserted their posts. As Gregory Orfalea has chronicled this episode in the area's history, at least 40,000 of the Lebanese deserters—Arabs who refused to fight for the Ottoman Empire against their own people—soon fled with their families to America.

They left the Bekaa Valley as depopulated and broken as Ireland was after the Great Potato Famine. Those who stayed faced a gnawing famine and a plague of locusts of biblical proportions. After World War I erupted, at least 100,000 Lebanese died of starvation, leaving the pastures, orchards, and vineyards of the Bekaa with far less than half the shepherds and grape pickers they had sheltered prior to the war.

I think of this history and of the stone from my grandmother's home whenever I read this passage from *Breath* by Lebanese American poet David Williams:

> The people I come from were thrown away
> as if they were nothing, whatever they might have
> said become stone, beyond human patience,
> except for the songs. But what is their daily
> breath against all the ardent, cunning
> justifications for murder?

These days I frequently hold that touchstone in the palm of my hand as I pray for peace and for what a lasting peace might mean for all the displaced people on this planet today. By some counts, political and economic refugees recently uprooted from their ancestral homelands now number two billion.

Let me take that statistical abstraction and strip it down for you. Wherever you travel in this world, it is likely that one out of every three people whose paths you cross are fleeing or have fled from their mother country. They are cultural and ecological orphans. They have been uprooted from the natal grounds in which their stories and songs, their environmental values and ethics, were first and most vividly nursed and nurtured. It is difficult to rekindle such sensibilities in a new place, surrounded by cultures and environmental constraints previously foreign to one.

We live during an era in which there are as many descendants of refugees around us as people who have *stayed put*, living in the same places where their ancestors have lived. Many of us who fit that description have endeavored long and hard to regain some sense of *nativity* in the places where we currently live; in many ways, it is the deepest struggle of my own life.

Although I savor the moments I've had crawling up the edges of limestone mesas with Hopi and Navajo neighbors who currently guide my attempts to live appropriately in a desert place, I also hear the reverberations of songs from *'a baladna*, the beloved ground that my grandfather referred to in English as simply "the Old Country." I am sometimes distracted when my Hopi and Navajo mentors attempt to teach me something about the land, for I am still grieving that I have never had the equivalent experience with my grandfather and grandmother in the land where they were born. A chain of *philopatry* has been broken, one that would otherwise connect me through their words and deeds to that ancestral land.

The Old Country. A place where on a hot day my grandfather could always find the shade of a centuries-old fig tree to rest beneath, where he could slowly savor the fruitiness of a fresh fig while watching the thousands of migratory waterfowl using the precious wetlands below the village. Above him, hawks and falcons would circle. Up on the slopes from the wetlands, he could hear lost lambs bleating longingly for their mothers. Kfar Zabad was the particular place that generated images and stories like this, ones my grandfather assumed he would pass on to my father, my father to me, and I to my children and nephews. They would be stories of belonging, not of ownership or control. They would carry with them the aural ecology of place, the oral history of family.

Instead, we have wailing, the songs of longing, not of be-longing. We hear the bleating of lost lambs.

II. Lambs Lost from Their Motherland

I am one of those lost lambs; you may well be one yourself. And yet I grew up thinking that my family and I were like most immigrants to the United States, relocating themselves in a different country to take advantage of all its economic and educational opportunities. In truth, most of my family fled from the oppressive Turks and a collapsed monoculture of mulberry cultivation for silk exporters, leaving Lebanon for the United States, Canada, Brazil, and Mexico a century ago. Early on it had never occurred to me that my ancestors were refugees *displaced* from their homes by the Ottoman War until another such conflict arose.

Then came the Six Days' War in 1967, when, among other things, Israel used U.S. military aid to take the Golan Heights from Syria, leaving another wave of refugees in its wake. I remember meeting one of those refugees right after that war, a sad, dark-haired orphan who arrived in the United States speaking only Arabic; after his parents had been killed, he was adopted by some Syrian American friends of my father. Although his foster parents spoke excellent Arabic, the boy himself hardly cared to speak his native language with them, it reminded him so much of his losses.

Forty years later, the July War—ostensibly between Israel and the Syrian-backed forces—created many more lost lambs in a matter of three weeks. This time it took place largely on Lebanese soil. My Lebanese cousins were suddenly awakened one dawn, tiny slivers of glass sparkling in their hair, when a bomb hit a ridge above their village, causing rock slides and sonic booms that knocked out every window in their home. Before another couple of nights had passed, hundreds of displaced Lebanese and Palestinians from other areas took refuge in the village. Within a few days, the bridges on the road between their farming village and the nearest cities had been demolished by missiles. The homes and fields of more than one hundred farming families in Kfar Zabad were left without outside food and water for ten days, forcing them to pump from the wetlands nearby in order to save their crops and their own lives as well. But the draining of the wetlands, otherwise managed through a traditional Islamic system of conservation called *hima*, further imperiled at least three species of endangered birds being monitored by the Society for the Protection of Nature in Lebanon.

As Asaad Serhal of the society later reported, one truck attempting to haul water from the wetlands to the Kfar Zabad fields was struck by a missile while it was still on the edge of the bird sanctuary: "At least one hundred farmers were affected. They couldn't move to harvest or load crops, because any pickup truck spotted by Israeli planes was immediately targeted, based on the assumption that it would be transporting weapons."

Fearing both the Syrian-backed and the Israeli forces, some of my cousins fled to the mountains in the north of Lebanon, hoping that they could escape the horrors. But they made the mistake of watching al-Jazeera and CNN on televisions in their friends' homes; seeing gunfire hit convoys of medical supplies and ambulances carrying the wounded, they realized no place was safe, no sanctuary inviolable, for people *or* for birds.

Whether we wish to admit it or not, many peoples, creatures, and places around the planet have been imperiled by what feels to them like another world war, but it is a war so diffuse that few call it that aloud. Wherever we now live—and most certainly in the United States, Iraq,

Lebanon, Israel, Indonesia, Iran, Afghanistan, Sudan, Spain, the Philippines, and the British Isles—we can hardly escape from the "news" of terror or of impending threats. We spend most of our waking hours in earshot of the latest reports of battles, suicide bombings, ambushes, and air raids. Despite media attempts to portray these incidents as isolated events, such conflicts cannot be so easily passed off as a series of unrelated, *low-intensity* skirmishes.

Let's be clear: an era of relative peace beginning with the close of the Vietnam War has been eclipsed by a period marked by bombings and bloodbaths. Whenever I hear of such tragedies hitting American *or* Arabian cities, I see this eclipse darkening the world around us. Regardless of how many casualties and refugees are already tallied by hospitals and relief agencies, many more people will be killed, wounded, and displaced unless we collectively yearn with all of our hearts for a different kind of news.

It must be news of certain peace, one in which people of many faiths and many colors are once again ensured the right to celebrate their own distinctive senses of place—not in exile, but with access to places they call *home*. To exercise the right to feel deeply placed in the world, each of us must give up using the labels that make a particular valley *my* homeland, but not yours, or that make you a member of "a chosen people" in a manner that excludes me or my kin.

If we are ever to return to peace, we have to shed our assumptions that true patriotism can in any way be based on domination, God-given preference, inheritance, and privilege purchased at the expense of others. We have to embrace a way of being with one another that ensures access to any sacred site or *motherland* by anyone who has spiritual roots there. Otherwise, such "places of the heart" will inevitably be torn apart by struggles for exclusive ownership and control.

III. Connecting Peace with the Right to Be in Place

Peace and *place*. I have always sensed that these two words have a bit of the same ring to them in modern English, but had not thought much about their deep connection until recently. I'm sure that the Middle English speakers who pronounced *peace* more like *pais* may have understood its resonance with the term for "place" in Spanish (*país*) and in French (*pays*). Today, we may seldom think about such phonetic and etymological linkages, but I have a hunch that most of us still feel them thrumming across our lips and in our hearts.

Oddly, I have seldom stopped to take note of the simplest of facts: that anyone who feels secure, grateful, and satisfied in a particular place is likely to feel *at peace*. Or that those who have fled war or other forms of violence are left not *in peace*, but in struggle. Not only do they grieve for what they have lost, but they may also have difficulty seeing the beauty of their newfound land because the salt of their own tears continues to blind them. They may feel humiliated by those who have taken over their homelands and may experience as their own any wounds that such lands have·suffered.

I have felt this palpable sort of grief among my Lebanese cousins who attempted to stay within the Bekaa Valley even when it became politically subdued, militarily occupied, and economically dominated by certain allies of the Syrian state. I remember the day I went to see pre-Roman ruins on a ridge above my grandparents' village, accompanied by my cousin Shibley Nabhan, who had earlier assisted with the archaeological sites survey in this area on behalf of the Lebanese government.

What had been intact temples with standing columns during his boyhood had become a jumble of bulldozed rubble by the time he took me back to one site he had mapped. He stood next to me on a ridge top, trying in vain to hold back the tears: "Those poor soldiers, they think all archaeology has hidden treasure—gold and silver they can sell. And so, in a manner of minutes, they uproot with their bulldozers what took decades to build, and *what stood here among us for thousands of·years without disturbance.*"

Less than a decade later Israeli jets dropped bombs on the same ridge, further damaging the archaeological sites that had already been looted by the Syrians. Additional bombs were dropped on a hill that stands just above the Kfar Zabad wetlands, which had been declared a migratory bird sanctuary of global importance. And yet Israeli missiles also targeted any farm truck that moved near those wetlands for nearly a month.

As I learned from William Dalrymple's award-winning memoir of his journey to holy sites in the Middle East, *From the Holy Mountain*, these insults to the sacred found in both natural and manmade places are not accidental, but instead have become intentional "commonplace" strategies during warfare. Soldiers have not been the only ones to destroy such antiquities and habitats. Over the past few decades, Jewish, Moslem, and Christian politicians have intentionally ordered the obliteration of the historic records and sacred sites belonging to other religious communities whose lands they now control. It is an attempt to change history by ethnic cleansing, to disrupt cultural attachments to place by ecological cleansing. When peace is shattered, the cultural memories that make *place* more than mere *space* are shattered as well.

I remember these lines from "The Clay's Memory," a poem by Salam al-Asadi, who was an eyewitness to the bombing of his hometown in southern Iraq before he fled and died as a refugee. As translated by Salih Altoma, they read:

> [T]hus we appear as a blend of tears and dust
> no distinction between our children's frightened eyes
> and the palm tree's wounds
> or between the silence of the schools' empty classrooms
> and the Euphrates' sad rumbling
> no difference between the bitter gasp, the sigh of
> withering souls
> the trees' smoke, the planes' thunder,
> and the veils of drowned women floating on the river's
> surface.

As I try to listen more deeply to the voices most often ignored in this world, much of what I hear is the keening of displaced peoples who feel they have been dismissed and rendered refugees unworthy of access to the lands they most deeply love. Humiliated, they struggle to regain some modicum of dignity, which they pray will come through reconnecting with their ancestral lands one day.

As the late Edward Said so eloquently observed, this is why we hear such desperation from Palestinian families evicted from their homes in the West Bank by Jewish settlers; they are humiliated because they do not currently have any legal recourse in Israeli courts to negotiate for a return to their land. And as my friend Sandy Tolan has documented in his fine book *The Lemon Tree*, some of the Israeli Jews who grew up in the houses of fleeing Palestinians have been told only of their *own* families' losses due to persecution and never of the Palestinian families whose homes they have acquired through an altogether different kind of persecution.

It is no wonder the world shudders every time it hears the anger of some 3.5 million Palestinians who have been evicted from their homes and forced to depart from their communities. This eviction may also be what underlies the vindictiveness seen in certain Kurds who have been forced back and forth between Turkey and Iraq, unable to retain control of land that has been the legacy of their families for centuries.

I hear the same mixture of indignation, grief, and anger from Navajo friends whose families were relocated against their wishes from the Big Mountain region of northern Arizona. They have been through years of bitter struggle against federal and tribal bureaucrats. The unfulfilled need to live *in peace and in place* was also what fueled the struggle against apartheid in South Africa and what continues to drive the Mayan farmers who feel that their only hope for staying on their land is to join ranks with Zapatista rebels in Chiapas.

For too long we have pretended that confronting racism and social injustice is an altogether different issue from safeguarding land rights, practicing multigenerational land stewardship, and protecting cultural and biological diversity. But in my own fieldwork as a conservation activist and ethnobiologist, I have seen these seemingly disparate threads woven tightly together nearly every place I go.

In Jerusalem, I participated in the first formal seed exchange of vegetables and herbs to which Israelis and Palestinians were invited. That evening a group known as Chefs for Peace—begun by an Armenian Christian named Kevork Alemian and an Iraqi-born Jew named Moshe Basson—cooked together and then broke bread together with their Palestinian Moslem friends at the same table. Whenever they cook together for public events, they pass all proceeds on to orphanages harboring children whose parents have perished in recent violence. They heal one another through sharing the place-based foods of the Holy Lands.

In the Sonoran Desert, I have worked on land-rights issues with descendants of the seminomadic Hia c-eḍ O'odham who used to have to drive past a sign in a national park in southern Arizona that warned tourists to "Watch Out for Cattle, Deer, and Indians." They were displaced from living near one of their sacred sites by preservationists who did not understand that the wildlife attracted to their desert oasis were lured there by the very habitats the O'odham themselves had stewarded for centuries. As such, the Hia c-eḍ O'odham are among hundreds of thousands of indigenous peoples who have been displaced from their homelands not only by wars between nation-states, but also by the development of national parks, resorts, and recreational areas used mostly by the rich.

Disturbed by such histories, for two years I worked with a multicultural team to assist displaced indigenous communities in their attempts to rectify such damage. We then delivered to hundreds of tribal leaders and human rights activists a portfolio called *Sacred Lands and Gathering Grounds: A Toolkit for Access, Protection, Restoration, and Co-management.* In the course of developing this portfolio, I realized that many native hunters, herders, and peasant farmers of desert landscapes on every continent have been treated by dominant societies as if they are ignorant, inferior, and lacking any permanent land rights; this environmental racism has resulted in the loss of both anciently managed cultural habitats and the biodiversity associated with them.

To avert such tragedies in the future, scholars around the world now bandy about the term *environmental justice*. But do the media or we ever use this concept as a lens to see and understand what is happening in Palestine, Iraq, Israel, Lebanon, and Afghanistan? What if we begin to view the crises in the Middle East not merely as economic and political struggles, but as ecological, ethical, and cultural ones as well?

Environmental injustice hurts individuals, disrupts their communities, and in a tragic way impairs their capacity to care adequately for one another and for the very land and waters that sustain them. The partial draining of the Kfar Zabad wetlands during a time of duress, when the war broke out in Lebanon, is one such ecological consequence of internecine strife and warfare. Making matters there even worse, refugees from Baalbek, Beirut, and southern Lebanon set up tent camps adjacent to the wetlands, amassing enormous amounts of solid waste in a matter of days. Were it not for the extraordinary effort by the Society for the Protection of Nature in Lebanon to provide relief to Kfar Zabad residents and refugees, the wetlands would have been further drained, contaminated, and degraded. Even as the bombing continued—while paved roads and bridges remained in disrepair—the society used its four-wheel-drive vehicles to ford wadis and deliver thirty tons of food and water to people stranded around the wetlands. Once this relief from a coalition of conservation groups arrived, Asaad Serhal found that the farmers were willing to halt their pumping and the refugees to refrain from dumping any more solid waste in the sanctuary: "The arrival of the shipment created marvels, for the community felt that we were there for them . . . they became very cooperative and started to pay more heed to our conservation concerns."

Mr. Serhal was not exaggerating about the farmers' cooperation. Barely two seasons later, when I arrived at the Kfar Zabad wetlands to meet Serhal's coworker, Dalia Al Jawhary, twenty farmers also showed up to meet us. Seven of them were my cousins, and one of them now volunteers at the wetlands as a birding guide. Their commitment runs deep.

That was not the last relief shipment—another thirty tons of supplies arrived soon after the July War cease-fire—nor was it the last of the discussions among conservationists, farmers, and refugees. Of course, more time is necessary to heal fully the wounds in Kfar Zabad, not only among the residents injured by bombing and famine, but also among the endangered birds and their habitats. Nevertheless, the Society for the Protection of Nature in Lebanon immediately heeded the principles of environmental justice that set all involved on the same path—a path that honors both human needs and the sacred lands about which we already care deeply.

Perhaps the path toward environmental justice begins by recognizing every person's and every peoples' right to peace and connection to place. I am reminded of the tenacity expressed in a few lines of the poem "I Belong There," written by Palestine's poet laureate Mahmoud Darwish:

> I belong there. I have memories. I was born as everyone is born.
> I have a mother, a house with many windows, brothers, friends, and a
>   prison cell with a chilly window! I have a wave snatched by
>   waterbirds, a panorama of my own.
> I have a saturated meadow. In the deep horizon of my word, I have a
>   moon, a bird's sustenance, and an immortal olive tree . . .
> I have learned and dismantled all the words in order to draw from them
>   a single word: *Home.*

IV. Listening to Arab Voices of the Land

We need to be reawakened to the possibilities of peace and place, to hear voices quite unlike our own that are pleading for these very same blessings. When I first heard that writer Laila ʿAllush describes herself as an

Arab Israeli, I became just as confused as most might be. But when I heard that one of her books of poetry is called *Spices on the Open Wound*, my confusion was transformed into pure curiosity and joy. Despite all the horrors 'Allush has witnessed in the Middle East, she has chosen to follow "the path of affection":

> . . . In the earth there was an apology for my father's wounds,
> And all along the bridges was my Arab countenance,
> In the tall poplars,
> In the trains and windows,
> In the smoke rings.
> Everything is Arab despite the change of tongue,
> Despite the trucks, cars, and the car lights . . .
> All the poplars and my ancestor's solemn orchards
> Were, I swear, smiling at me with Arab affection.
> Despite all that had been eliminated and coordinated and the "modern" sounds . . .
> Despite the seas of light and technology . . .
> O my grandparents, the rich soil was bright with Arab reserve,
> And it sang out, believe me, with affection.

What I love about this poem is that no one can take away 'Allush's affection for the land—*or its affection for those who have cared for it*. The land may become occupied, its wetlands temporarily drained, and its fields and hedgerows temporarily starved of water, but it will still persist in ways that people love in their dreams and in their hearts. Should anyone attempt to reforge their deep bond with the land, there can be a healing of the most horrific wounds and the possibility of a return of the "brightness" that can be found in any land-based culture.

I was surprised to hear how quickly after the cessation of the war in Lebanon that the people of Kfar Zabad were able to set aside their grief in order to express their affection for the land once more. Less than two months after the threat to the community's very existence, "Peace and Birds" festivals were held in both Kfar Zabad and Ebel es-Saqi, another important bird area in southern Lebanon. In Kfar Zabad, more than 150 members of the local community—including twenty-five farmers—came out to clean up the wetlands' edges, to develop an action plan for farmer participation in wetland protection, to feast on traditional foods, and to celebrate the fact that three endangered bird species had not been made into refugees! The irony of the event was not lost on a reporter for a major Lebanese newspaper, the *Daily Star*:

> Kfar Zbad had [already] become an experiment in a different kind of environmental protection policy, home-grown and community-based. Now, with the eruption of another war in Lebanon and the arrival of another postwar reconstruction period—arguably more threatening to the environment than the war itself—Kfar Zabad might become an experiment all over again, this time illustrating how nature conservation strategies make for markedly more efficient responses to crisis management and humanitarian relief.

After I had sauntered around the Kfar Zbad hima with the farmers involved in restoring the wetlands so that migratory waterfowl might take refuge there, I remembered a poem that spoke of farmers engaged with the flight of another "migrant." It was an unidentified flying object that once landed a couple hundred kilometers away from Kfar Zabad on the rural outskirts of Damascus. In the poem "The Bomb That Fell on Uncle Abdu's Farm" by Gregory Orfalea—whose family hails from Zahle, not far from Kfar Zabad—we hear of the kind of resilience required to make peace and restoration last in the places we love:

> The Phantoms approached, we were told,
>   like warps in the sky, like gossip,
>   gone real, aimed in steel,
>   at the eyes of the village.
>
> All the farmers and farmers' boys ran
>   to the rooftops and watched,
>   for it was terrifying
>   and beautiful to see a wedge
>   of silver up from the South.
>
> And they began to fall with a
>   vengeance, under the anti-air-
>   craft that ringed Damascus and the
>   villagers whooped for there seemed
>   a magic field around their fields.
>
> Until a cow-shed flew in red to the sky,
>   and a mother milking collapsed
>   in her milk. The milk ran pink.

Next door, in my great-uncle's newly
     Irrigated fields, a bomb fell.
               The mud smothered it. The mud
                    talked to it. The mud wrapped
                         its death like a mother. And
                    the bomb with American lettering
                         did not go off.

Water your garden always. Always.

References

Chapter 1. Camel Whisperers

Barnard, William C. (Associated Press). [1940s]. Hi Jolly and the U.S. Camel Corps: Prospector convinced Arizona still has camels.

Bell, Fillman, Keith Anderson, and Yvonne Stewart. 1980. *Quitobaquito Cemetery and Its History.* National Park Service Western Archaeological Center, Tucson, Ariz.

Boyd, Eva Jolene. 1995. *Noble Brutes: Camels on the American Frontier.* Republic of Texas Press, Plano.

Bryson, Jack. 1964. America's cameleers. *Desert Magazine* 27 (8): 26–28.

Day, James M. 1976. Paragons of patience: Texas camel mythology. The Greater Llano Estacado Southwest. *Heritage Quarterly* 6 (3): 11–16.

Emmett, Chris. 1932. *Texas Camel Tales.* Naylor, San Antonio, Tex.

Faulk, Odie B. 1976. *The U.S. Camel Corps: An Army Experiment.* Oxford University Press, New York.

Fontana, Bernard. 2003. Introduction. In *Borderman: Memoirs of Federico José María Ronstadt,* edited by Edward F. Ronstadt, xxiii–xxxi. University of Arizona Press, Tucson.

Fowler, Harlan D. 1950. *Camels to California.* Stanford University Press, Menlo Park, Calif.

Frangos, Steve. 2000. Philip Tedro: A Greek legend in the American West. *Greek American Review* 10. Available at http://www.hellenicomserve.com/ philiptedro.html.

Government camels imported to explore the Great American Desert. 1885. *Arizona Gazette,* October 8, 3.

Hi Jolly, the Greek who came to Arizona with camels. 1883. *Prescott (Weekly) Courier,* September 1, 1.

Lesley, Lewis B. 2006. The purchase and importation of camels by the United States government, 1855–1857. *Southwestern Historical Quarterly Online* 33 (1). Available at http://www.tsha.utexas.edu/publications/journals/ shq/online/vo33/n1/contrib._DIV L395.html.

Malis, Sean. 2007. The mythical Fort Tejon Camel Corps. Fort Tejon Historical Association. Available at http://www.forttejon.org/camels. Accessed May 19, 2007.

Murbarger, Nell. 1948. Trouble shooter for the Camel Corps. *Scenic Southwest* (July): 5, 10, 18.

Nabhan, Gary, Wendy Hodgson, and Frances Fellows. 1989. A meager living on lava and sand? Hia C-eḍ O'odham food resources and habitat diversity in oral and documentary histories. *Journal of the Southwest* 31 (4): 508–33.

Obermüller, Joseph L. Life and times of a mining engineer, 1864–1947. Arizona Historical Society archives, MS 593, Tucson.

Orfalea, Gregory. 2006. *The Arab Americans: A History.* Olive Branch Press and Interlink, Northhampton, Mass.

Stammerjohan, George. 2007. The camel experiment in California. Fort Tejon Historical Association. Available at http://www.forttejon.org/camels. Accessed May 19, 2007.

Wagoner, J. Jay. 1975. *Early Arizona: Prehistory to Civil War.* University of Arizona Press, Tucson.

Winsor, Mulford. 1945. Hi-Jolly. Arizona Historical Society archives, MS 636.295, May 1945 typescript, Tucson.

Yancey, Diane. 1995. *Camels for Uncle Sam.* Hendrick-Long, Dallas, Tex.

Chapter 2. ¿Eres Paisano?

Banqueri, Josef Antonio, trans. 1988. *Libro de agricultura del doctor excelente Abu Zacariua Iahia.* 2 vols. 1802. Reprint. Clásicos Agrarios series. Ministerio de Agricultura, Pesca y Alimentación, Seville, Spain.

Barquet, Patricia Jacobs. 2000. *Diccionario enciclopédico de Mexicanos de origen libanés y de otros pueblos del Levante.* Ediciones del Ermitaño, Mexico City.

Bayless, Rick, Deann Groen Bayless, and Jean Marie Brownson. 1996. *Rick Bayless's Mexican Kitchen.* Scribner's, New York.

Crosby, Alfred C., Jr. 1972. *The Columbian Exchange: Biological and Cultural Consequences of 1492.* Greenwood Press, Westport, Conn.

Dunmire, William. 2004. *Gardens of New Spain: How Mediterranean Plants and Foods Changed America.* University of Texas Press, Austin.

Gilitz, David M. 2002. *Secrecy and Deceit: The Religion of the Crypto-Jews.* University of New Mexico Press, Albuquerque.

Jaramillo, Cleofas M. 1981. *The Genuine New Mexico Tasty Recipes (Potajas Sabrosas).* 1939. Reprint. Ancient City Press, Santa Fe.

Mardam-Bey, Farouk. 2002. *Ziryab: Authentic Arab Cuisine.* Ici La Press, Woodbury, Conn.

Menocal, María Rosa. 2002. *Ornament of the World: How Muslims, Jews, and Christians Created a Culture of Tolerance in Medieval Spain.* Little, Brown, Boston.

Salloum, Habeeb. 2007. Ziryab: A social trendsetter missing from the Western Hall of Fame. Unpublished manuscript, Toronto, Ontario (in author's possession).

Trablousi, Fawzaz. 2007. *A History of Modern Lebanon.* Pluto Press, London.

Chapter 3. Chasing Alice Ann

Adams, Ramon F. 1998. *Western Words: A Dictionary of the Old West.* Hippocrene Press, New York.

Biggers, Jeff. 2006. *In the Sierra Madre.* University of Illinois Press, Urbana.

Broyles, Bill, Luke Evans, Richard S. Felger, and Gary Paul Nabhan. 1997. Our grand desert: A gazetteer for northwestern Sonora, southwestern Arizona, and northeastern Baja California. *Journal of the Southwest* 39 (3–4): 703–856. Reprinted in *Dry Borders: Great Natural Reserves of the Sonoran Desert*, edited by Richard Stephen Felger and Bill Broyles, 581–679. University of Utah Press, Salt Lake City, 2006.

Mathiot, Madeleine. 1973–76. *A Dictionary of Papago Usage*. 2 vols. Indiana University Monographs in Linguistics, Bloomington, Indiana.

Nabhan, Gary Paul. 2007. Arabic in the Saddle. *Saudi Aramco World* 58 (2) (March–April). Available at http://www.saudiaramcoworld.com.

Nabhan, Gary Paul, and Luciano Noriega. In press. Flora and ethnobotany of Quitovac, a Sonoran Desert oasis. In *Ecology and Conservation of Springs in North America*, edited by Lawrence E. Stevens and Vicki J. Meretsky. Arizona-Sonora Desert Museum Studies in Natural History. University of Arizona Press, Tucson.

Salloum, Habeeb. Arabic contributions to the Spanish language. Available at http://www .alhewar.net/Basket/Habeeb_Salloum_Spanish_Language.htm.

Saxton, Dean, Lucille Saxton, and Susie Enos. 1985. *A Papago/English Dictionary*. University of Arizona Press, Tucson.

Smead, Robert N. 2004. *Vocabulario Vaquero / Cowboy Talk: A Dictionary of Spanish Terms from the American West*. University of Oklahoma Press, Norman.

Sobrazo, Horacio. 1963. *Vocabulario sonorense*. Editorial Porrua, Mexico City.

Chapter 4. Oasis Time

Blottière, Alain. 2000. *Siwa: The Oasis*. Harpocrates, Alexandria, Egypt.

Blunt, Wilfred Scawen. 1903. *The Seven Golden Odes of Pagan Arabia*. Translated from Arabic by Lady Anne Blunt. Chiswick Press, London.

Colley, Charles. 1977. *The Century of Robert Forbes: The Career of a Pioneer Agriculturalist, Agronomist, Environmentalist, Conservationist, and Water Specialist in Arizona and Beyond*. Arizona Historical Society, Tucson.

Forbes, Robert. 1920. Siwa Oasis. *Cairo Scientific Journal* 10: 4–9.

Forbes, Robert. 1921. Agriculture in the Sahara. Typescript. Arizona Historical Society archives, MS 0261, Tucson, with note that it was published in *The Republican* (the *Arizona Republic*), January 9.

Forbes, Robert H. 1956. Laura Kerman, her life story. Typescript. Arizona Historical Society archives, MS 0261, Tucson.

Nabhan, Gary Paul. 1982. *The Desert Smells Like Rain*. North Point Press, Berkeley, Calif.

Nabhan, Gary Paul. 2001. Agrobiodiversity change in a Saharan Desert oasis, 1919–2006: Historic shifts in Tasiwit (Berber) and Bedouin crop inventories of Siwa, Egypt. *Economic Botany* 61 (1): 31–43.

Nabhan, Gary Paul. In press. Plant diversity influenced by indigenous management of freshwater springs: Flora of Quitovac, Sonora, Mexico. In *Ecology and Conservation of Springs in North America*, edited by Lawrence Stevens and Vickie J. Meretsky. Arizona-Sonora Desert Museum Studies in Natural History. University of Arizona Press, Tucson.

Nabhan, Gary Paul, Amadeo Rea, Eric Mellink, Karen Reichhardt, and Charles Hutchinson. 1982. Papago influences on habitat and biotic diversity: Quitovac ethnoecology. *Journal of Ethnobiology* 2: 124–43.

Chapter 5. That Cosmopolitan Look

Bircher, Alfred G., and Warda H. Bircher. 2000. *Encyclopedia of Fruit Trees and Edible Flowering Plants in Egypt and the Subtropics*. American University of Cairo Press, Cairo.

Boulos, Loufty, and M. Nabil el-Hadidi. 1994. *The Weed Flora of Egypt*. American University of Cairo Press, Cairo.

Davidson, Alan. 1999. *The Oxford Companion to Food*. Oxford University Press, Oxford.

Diamond, Jared. 1997. *Guns, Germs, and Steel: The Fates of Human Society*. W. W. Norton, New York.

Hobbs, Joseph J. 1989. *Bedouin Life in the Egyptian Wilderness*. University of Texas Press, Austin.

Kunstler, James Howard. 1994. *The Geography of Nowhere: The Rise and Decline of America's Man-Made Landscapes*. Free Press, New York.

Morrow, Susan Brind. 1997. *The Names of Things: Life, Language, and Beginnings in the Egyptian Desert*. Riverhead Books and Penguin-Putnam, New York.

Nabhan, Gary Paul, Patricia West, Richard S. Felger, Mary O'Brien, Josh O'Brien, Thomas R. Van Devender, Ana Lilia Reina Guerrero, Steven P. McLaughlin, Phil Jenkins, and Juliet C. Stromberg. 2002. Appendix B: Naturalized Exotic Species in the Sonoran Desert Region: Flora. In *Invasive Exotic Species in the Sonoran Region*, edited by Barbara Tellman, 346–55. Arizona-Sonora Desert Museum Studies in Natural History. University of Arizona Press, Tucson.

Pollan, Michael. 2002. *The Botany of Desire: A Plant's Eye View of the World*. Random House, New York.

Quammen, David. 1998. Planet of weeds: Tallying the losses of Earth's plants and animals. *Harper's Magazine* (October): 57–69.

Rindos, David. 1984. *The Origins of Agriculture: An Evolutionary Perspective*. Academic Press, New York.

Stark, Freya. 1936. *The Southern Gates of Arabia*. Tarcher and Houghton-Mifflin, Los Angeles.

Stevens, Lawrence E., and Tina Ayers. 2002. The biodiversity and distribution of exotic vascular plants and animals in the Grand Canyon region. In *Invasive Exotic Species in the Sonoran Region*, edited by Barbara Tellman, 241–65. Arizona-Sonora Desert Museum Studies in Natural History. University of Arizona Press, Tucson.

Terrill, Ceiridwen. 2007. *Unnatural Landscapes: Tracking Invasive Species*. University of Arizona Press, Tucson.

Chapter 6. A Desert Is a Home That Has Migrated

Ashtiany, Julia. 1990. *Abbasid Belles-Lettres: Cambridge History of Arabic Literature*. Vol. 2. Cambridge University Press, Cambridge. (This volume includes the Bashār ibn Burd poem, first technically translated into English by A. H. L. Beeston, p. 280, freely translated here.)

Brown, John Permain. 1969. *The Lebanon and Phoenicia: Ancient Texts Illustrating Their Physical Geography and Native Industries*. Vol. 1. American University of Beirut, Beirut.

Casson, L., trans. 1989. *The Periplus of the Erythraen Sea*. Princeton University Press, Princeton, N.J.

Chittick, Neville. 1969. A new look at the history of Pate. *Journal of African History* 10 (3): 375–91.

Dalby, Andrew. 2000. *Dangerous Tastes: The Story of Spices*. University of California Press, Berkeley and Los Angeles.

Gil, Moshe. 1992. *A History of Palestine, 634 to 1099*. Cambridge University Press, Cambridge.

Haddad, G. F. 2006. Scholars: Imam al-Qadi Yusuf al-Nabhani. Available at http://www.sunnah.org/history/Scholars/al-Nabhani.

Hourani, Albert. 1991. *A History of the Arab Peoples*. Belknap Press of Harvard University Press, Cambridge, Mass.

Kennedy, Hugh. 2004. *The Court of the Caliphs: When Baghdad Ruled the Moslem World*. Phoenix/Orion Books, London.

Menon, Bala. 1999. The magic of Bahla. Available at http://www.geocities.com/Athens/Acropolis/3763/Bahla.htm?20064.

al-Naboodah, Hasan M. 1997. The Banu Nabhan in the Omani sources. In *New Arabic Studies*, vol. 4, edited by G. Rex Smith, J. R. Smart, and B. R. Pridham, 181–95. University of Exeter Press, Exeter, England.

Omani Minister of Foreign Affairs. 2006. Nabahana's rule. Available at http://www.mofa.gov.om/oman/discoveroman/omanhistory/NabahanRule.

Orfalea, Gregory. 1988. *Before the Flames: A Quest for the History of Arab Americans*. University of Texas Press, Austin.

Simarski, Lynn Teo. 1991. Fortified Oman. *Saudi Aramco World* 42 (1) (January–February). Available at http://www.saudiaramcoworld.com/issue1991. fortified.oman.

Sughairoon, Ibrahim el-Zain. 1995. *Oman in History*. Minister of Information, Muscat, Oman. Excerpted at http://www.omanet.om/english/history/ overview.asp. Accessed May 28, 2007.

Ṣuhar: Regnal chronologies. 2007. Available at http://www.hostkingdom.net/Arabia/htm/#suhar. Accessed April 29, 2007.

Turner, Jack. 2004. *Spice: The History of a Temptation*. Vintage Books, New York.

Waeti, John, ed. In press. *Date Cultivars of the Sultanate of Oman*. Fruit Science, vol. 2. Minister of Information, Sultanate of Oman, Muscat. Available at http://www.1902-encyclopedia.com/A/ARA/arabia-25.htm.

Wilson, Sir Arnold Talbot. 1928. *The Persian Gulf*. George Allen and Unwin, London.

Chapter 7. Watching for Sign, Tasting the Mountain Thyme

Deming, Alison Hawthorne, and Lauret E. Savoy, eds. 2002. *The Colors of Nature: Culture, Identity, and the Natural World.* Milkweed Editions, Minneapolis–St. Paul, Minn.

Linhart, Yan B. 1999. Thyme is of the essence: Biochemical polymorphism and multiple species deterrence. *Evolutionary Ecology Research* 1: 151–71.

Nabhan, Gary Paul. 2002a. Cultural dispersals of plants and animals to the midriff islands of the Sea of Cortés: Integrating indigenous human dispersal agents into island biogeography. *Journal of the Southwest* 42 (3): 545–58.

Nabhan, Gary Paul. 2002b. Listening for the ancient tones, watching for sign, tasting for the mountain thyme. In *The Colors of Nature: Culture, Identity, and the Natural World,* edited by Alison Hawthorne Deming and Larel E. Savoy, 190–98. Milkweed Editions, Minneapolis–St. Paul, Minn.

Nabhan, Gary Paul. 2003. *Singing the Turtles to Sea: The Comcáac (Seri) Art and Science of Reptiles.* University of California Press, Berkeley and Los Angeles.

Wardini, Elie. 2002. *Orientalia Lovaniensia Analecta: Lebanese Place-Names, a Typology of Regional Variation and Continuity.* Ultgeverij Peters, Paris.

Chapter 8. Hummingbirds and Human Aggression

Broyles, Bill. 2006. *Sunshot: Peril and Wonder in the Gran Desierto.* University of Arizona Press, Tucson.

Calder, William A., III, ed. 1983. Site-fidelity, longevity, and population dynamics of Broad-Tailed Hummingbirds: A ten year study. *Oecologia* 56: 359–68.

Carothers, Andre. 1991. After the storm: The deluge. *Greenpeace Magazine* (October–December): 17.

Cox, John. 1991. Waging war against the Earth. *Environmental Action* (March–April): 2–3.

Hoy, Wilton. 1970. *Organ Pipe Historical Research.* Organ Pipe Cactus National Monument, Lukeville, Ariz.

Kroeber, Clifton B., and Bernard L. Fontana. 1987. *Massacre on the Gila: An Account of the Last Major Battle Between American Indians.* University of Arizona Press, Tucson.

Lyon, David L., James Crandall, and Mark McCone. 1977. A test of the adaptiveness of interspecific territoriality in the Blue-Throated Hummingbird. *The Auk* 94 (3): 448–49.

Montagu, Ashley. 1976. *The Nature of Human Aggression.* Oxford University Press, New York.

al-Naboodah, Hasan M. 1997. The Banu Nabhan in the Omani sources. In *New Arabian Studies,* vol. 4, edited by G. Rex Smith, J. R. Smart, and B. R. Pridham, 181–95. University of Exeter, Exeter, England.

Pumpelly, Raphael. 1870. *Across Asia and America.* Leypoldt and Holt, New York.

Pumpelly, Raphael. 1918. *My Reminisces.* Henry Holt, New York.

Roosevelt, Kermit. 1920. *Happy Hunting-Grounds.* Charles Scribner's Sons, New York.

Tavris, Carol. 1982. *Anger: The Misunderstood Emotion.* Touchstone Books of Simon and Schuster, New York.

Underhill, Ruth. 1939. *Social Organization of the Papago Indians*. Columbia University Press, New York.

Wardini, Elie. 2002. *Orientalia Lovaniensia Analecta: Lebanese Place-Names, a Typology of Regional Variation and Continuity*. Ultgeverij Peters, Paris.

Wilson, Sir Arnold Talbot. 1928. *The Persian Gulf*. George Allen and Unwin, London.

Wilson, Edward O. 1978. *On Human Nature*. Harvard University Press, Cambridge, Mass.

Chapter 9. Other Voices, Human and Avian

'Allush, Laila. 2001. The path of affection. Translated by Abdelwahab M. Elmessiri. In *The Poetry of Arab Women*, edited by Nathalie Handel, 78–79. Interlink Books, New York.

al-Asadi, Salam. 2003. Clay's memory. Translated by Salih Altoma. In *Poets Against the War*, edited by Sam Hamill, 15–16. Thunder's Mouth Press and Nation Books, New York.

Dalrymple, William. 1999. *From the Holy Mountain: A Journey among Christians of the Middle East*. Henry Holt, New York.

Darwish, Mahmoud. 2003. I belong there. Translated by Munir Akash and Carolyn Forché. In *Unfortunately, It Was Paradise*, edited by Munir Akash and Carolyn Forché, 7–8. University of California Press, Berkeley and Los Angeles.

al-Khatib, Bassima. 2006. Aid helps protect Lebanese IBA [Important Bird Area]. *BirdLife International* (November 15). Available at http://www. iucn.org/places/wescana/news.

Kilani, Hala. 2006. The power of the [World Conservation] Union to achieve conservation demonstrated during war on Lebanon. October 11. Available at http://www.iucn.org/places/wescana/hima.html.

Lebanese children camp for peace and birds. 2006. *BirdLife International* (October 20). Available at http://www.middle-east-online.com/English/ ?id=17985.

Orfalea, Gregory. 1988. *Before the Flames: A Quest for the History of Arab Americans*. University of Texas Press, Austin.

Orfalea, Gregory. 2000. The bomb that fell on Abdu's farm. In *Grape Leaves: A Century of Arab-American Poetry*, edited by Gregory Orfalea and Sharif Elmusa, 260–61. Interlink Books, New York.

Said, Edward. 2000. The Middle-East "peace process": Misleading implications and brutal realities. In *The Edward Said Reader*, edited by Moustafa Bayoumi and Andrew Rubin, 382–98. Vintage, New York.

Seibert, David, Gary Paul Nabhan, Laurie Monti, Karen Jarrett-Ziemski, and Eunice Tso. 2004. *Sacred Lands and Gathering Grounds: A Toolkit for Access, Protection, Restoration, and Co-management*. Center for Sustainable Environments of Northern Arizona University, Flagstaff.

Tolan, Sandy. 2006. *The Lemon Tree: An Arab, a Jew, and the Heart of the Middle East*. Bloomsbury USA, New York.

Williams, David. 1993. *Breath: Traveling Mercies*. Alice James Books, Cambridge, Mass.

Source Credits

"Camel Whisperers: Desert Nomads Crossing Paths" will appear in a slightly different form in *Journal of Arizona History* in 2008. "Chasing Alice Ann: Arabic Terms Leaping Languages and Oceans" was excerpted as "Arabic in the Saddle," *Saudi Aramco World* 58 (2) (March–April 2007) (available at http://www.saudiaramcoworld.com). An earlier version of "A Desert Is a Home That Has Migrated" is given at http://www.garynabhan.com. "Watching for Sign, Tasting the Mountain Thyme" first appeared as "Listening for the Ancient Tones, Watching for Sign, Tasting for the Mountain Thyme," in *The Colors of Nature: Culture, Identity, and the Natural World*, edited by Alison Hawthorne Deming and Lauret E. Savoy, 190–98 (Milkweed Editions, Minneapolis–St. Paul, 2002). "Hummingbirds and Human Aggression: A View from High Tanks" first appeared in *Georgia Review* 51 (summer 1992): 213–32, and was republished in *Cultures of Habitat*, by Gary Paul Nabhan, 112–32 (Counterpoint Press, Washington, D.C., 1997). "Other Voices, Human and Avian: Reconnecting Place with Peace in a Broken World" first appeared as "Listening to the Other," *Orion* magazine (May–June 2002): 18–27.

About the Author

An Arab American, Gary Paul Nabhan has done field research on the conservation and culinary uses of desert plants for a quarter century in the United States, Mexico, Lebanon, Oman, and Egypt. He has been honored with a MacArthur "Genius" Award, a Lannan Literary Fellowship, and a Lifetime Achievement Award from the Society for Conservation Biology. Nabhan is the author, editor, or coauthor of twenty books, three of which have won national or international awards. He has also served on the board of the Arab-American Writer's Guild known as al-RAWI. He was the founding director of the Center for Sustainable Environments at Northern Arizona University before returning to his desert home near Tucson, where he is now affiliated with the Southwest Center of the University of Arizona. See www.garynabhan.com.

Library of Congress Cataloging-in-Publication Data

Nabhan, Gary Paul.
  Arab/American : landscape, culture, and cuisine in
two great deserts / Gary Paul Nabhan.
      p. cm.
  Includes bibliographical references and index.
  ISBN 978-0-8165-2658-1 (hardcover : alk. paper) —
ISBN 978-0-8165-2659-8 (pbk. : alk. paper)
    1. Southwest, New—Civilization. 2. Civilization, Arab.
3. Southwest, New—Social life and customs. 4. Arab
countries—Social life and customs. 5. Cookery,
American—Southwestern style. 6. Cookery, Arab.
7. Deserts—Social aspects—Southwest, New.
8. Deserts—Social aspects—Arab countries. 9. Nabhan,
Gary Paul—Homes and haunts—Southwest, New.
10. Arab Americans—Southwest, New—Social life
and customs. I. Title.
F787.N33 2008
979—dc22   2007033781